U·X·L
ENCYCLOPEDIA OF
LANDFORMS
AND OTHER GEOLOGIC FEATURES

DATE DUE

BRODART, CO.

Cat. No. 23-221-003

U·X·L

ENCYCLOPEDIA OF
LANDFORMS
AND OTHER GEOLOGIC FEATURES

3

Ocean basin
Plain
Plateau
Stream and river
Valley
Volcano

Rob Nagel

™

GALE

Detroit • New York • San Diego • San Francisco • Cleveland • New Haven, Conn. • Waterville, Maine • London • Munich

U•X•L Encyclopedia of Landforms and Other Geologic Features

Rob Nagel

Project Editor
Diane Sawinski

Permissions
Lori Hines

Imaging and Multimedia
Robyn Young

Product Design
Michelle DiMercurio

Composition
Evi Seoud

Manufacturing
Rita Wimberley

Library of Congress Cataloging-in-Publication Data
Nagel, Rob.
    UXL encyclopedia of landforms and other geologic features / Rob Nagel.
        p. cm.
            Summary: Explores the physical structure of the Earth's landforms, including what they are, how they look, how they were created and change over time, and major geological events associated with each.
            Includes bibliographical references (p.xxix).
            ISBN 0-7876-7611-X (set hardcover) — ISBN 0-7876-7670-5 (Volume 1) — ISBN 0-7876-7671-3 (Volume 2) — ISBN 0-7876-7672-1 (Volume 3)
            1. Landforms—Encyclopedias, Juvenile. 2. Physical geography—Encyclopedias, Juvenile. [1. Landforms—Encyclopedias. 2. Physical geography—Encyclopedias.] I. Title: Encyclopedia of landforms and other geologic features. II. Title.
    GB406.N35 2003
    551.41'03—dc22   2003014898

Contents

Reader's Guide

From the perspective of human time, very little changes on the surface of Earth. From the perspective of geologic time, the period from Earth's beginning more than 4.5 billion years ago to the present day, however, the surface of the planet is in constant motion, being reshaped over and over. The constructive and destructive forces at play in this reshaping have helped create landforms, specific geomorphic features on Earth's land surface. Mountains and canyons, plains and plateaus, faults and basins: These are but a few of the varied and spectacular features that define the landscape of the planet.

U•X•L Encyclopedia of Landforms and Other Geologic Features explores twenty-two of these landforms: what they are, how they look, how they were created, how they change over time, and major geological events associated with them.

Scope and Format

In three volumes, *U•X•L Encyclopedia of Landforms and Other Geologic Features* is organized alphabetically into the following chapters:

Basin	Canyon
Cave	Coast and shore
Continental margin	Coral reef
Delta	Dune and other desert features
Fault	Floodplain
Geyser and hot spring	Glacial landforms and features
Landslide and other gravity movements	Mesa and butte

Meteorite crater   Mountain

Ocean basin   Plain

Plateau   Stream and river

Valley   Volcano

Each chapter begins with an overview of that specific landform. The remaining information in the chapter is broken into four sections:

- **The shape of the land** describes the physical aspects of the landform, including its general size, shape, and location on the surface of the planet, if applicable. A standard definition of the landform opens the discussion. If the landform exists as various types, those types are defined and further described.

- **Forces and changes: Construction and destruction** describes in detail the forces and agents responsible for the construction, evolution, and destruction of the landform. The erosional actions of wind and water, the dynamic movement of crustal plates, the influence of gravity, and the changes in climate both across regions and time are explained in this section, depending on their relation to the specific landform.

- **Spotlight on famous forms** describes specific examples of the landform in question. Many of these examples are well-known; others may not be. The biggest, the highest, and the deepest were not the sole criteria for selection, although many of the featured landforms meet these superlatives. While almost all chapters include examples found in the United States, they also contain examples of landforms found throughout the world.

- **For More Information** offers students further sources for research—books or Web sites—about that particular landform.

Other features include more than 120 color photos and illustrations, "Words to Know" boxes providing definitions of terms used in each chapter, sidebar boxes highlighting interesting facts relating to particular landforms, a general bibliography, and a cumulative index offering easy access to all of the subjects discussed in *U•X•L Encyclopedia of Landforms and Other Geologic Features*.

Acknowledgments

A note of appreciation is extended to *U•X•L Encyclopedia of Landforms and Other Geologic Features* advisors, who provided helpful suggestions when this work was in its formative stages:

Chris Cavette, Science Writer, Fremont, California

Mark Crawford, Geologist, Madison, Wisconsin

Elizabeth Jackson, Adams Elementary School, Cary, North Carolina

Kate Plieth, Fitzgerald High School, Warren, Michigan

Susan Spaniol, Hillside Middle School, Farmington Hills, Michigan

The author would like to extend special thanks to geologist and writer Mark Crawford and science writer Chris Cavette for their insightful critiques and comments on the table of contents and on the material in each chapter. The advice of Mr. Crawford, in particular, proved invaluable.

Thanks are also extended to U•X•L publisher Tom Romig and product manager Julia Furtaw for developing this title and offering it to the author. Working with the entire U•X•L staff has always been a distinct pleasure.

Finally, and most important, the author would like to offer warm and gracious thanks to U•X•L senior editor Diane Sawinski. Without her guidance, enthusiasm, and tireless effort, this work would not appear as it does.

Comments and Suggestions

We welcome your comments on *U•X•L Encyclopedia of Landforms and Other Geologic Features*. Please write: Editors, *U•X•L Encyclopedia of Landforms and Other Geologic Features*, U•X•L, 27500 Drake Rd., Farmington Hills, MI 48331; call toll-free: 1-800-877-4253; fax: 248-699-8097; or send e-mail via http://www.gale.com.

Geologic Timescale

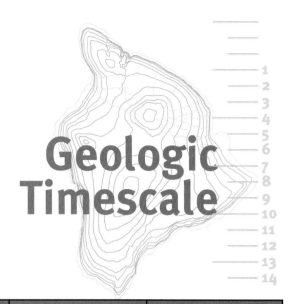

Era	Period		Epoch	Started (millions of years ago)
Cenozoic: 66.4 millions of years ago–present time	Quaternary		Holocene	0.01
			Pleistocene	1.6
	Tertiary	Neogene	Pliocene	5.3
			Miocene	23.7
		Paleogene	Oligocene	36.6
			Eocene	57.8
			Paleocene	66.4
Mesozoic: 245–66.4 millions of years ago	Cretaceous		Late	97.5
			Early	144
	Jurassic		Late	163
			Middle	187
			Early	208
	Triassic		Late	230
			Middle	240
			Early	245
Paleozoic: 570–245 millions of years ago	Permian		Late	258
			Early	286
	Carboniferous	Pennsylvanian	Late	320
		Mississippian	Early	360
	Devonian		Late	374
			Middle	387
			Early	408
	Silurian		Late	421
			Early	438
	Ordovician		Late	458
			Middle	478
			Early	505
	Cambrian		Late	523
			Middle	540
			Early	570
Precambrian time: 4500-570 millions of years ago				4500

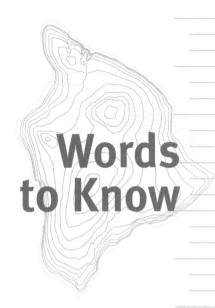

Words to Know

A

Ablation zone: The area of a glacier where mass is lost through melting or evaporation at a greater rate than snow and ice accumulate.

Abrasion: The erosion or wearing away of bedrock by continuous friction caused by sand or rock fragments in water, wind, and ice.

Abyssal hill: A gently sloping, small hill, typically of volcanic origin, found on an abyssal plain.

Abyssal plain: The relatively flat area of an ocean basin between a continental margin and a mid-ocean ridge.

Accretionary wedge: A mass of sediment and oceanic rock that is transferred from an oceanic plate to the edge of the less dense plate under which it is subducting.

Accumulation zone: The area of a glacier where mass is increased through snowfall at a greater rate than snow and ice is lost through ablation.

Active continental margin: A continental margin that has a very narrow, or even nonexistent, continental shelf and a narrow and steep continental slope that ends in a deep trench instead of a continental rise; it is marked by earthquake and volcanic activity.

Alluvial fan: A fanlike deposit of sediment that forms where an intermittent, yet rapidly flowing canyon or mountain stream spills out onto a plain or relatively flat valley.

Alluvium: A general term for sediment (rock debris such as gravel, sand, silt, and clay) deposited by running water.

Alpine glacier: A relatively small glacier that forms in high elevations near the tops of mountains.

Angle of repose: The steepest angle at which loose material on a slope remains motionless.

Anticline: An upward-curving (convex) fold in rock that resembles an arch.

Arête: A sharp-edged ridge of rock formed between adjacent cirque glaciers.

Arroyo: A steep-sided and flat-bottomed gully in a dry region that is filled with water for a short time only after occasional rains.

Asteroid: A small, irregularly shaped rocky body that orbits the Sun.

Asthenosphere: The section of the mantle immediately beneath the lithosphere that is composed of partially melted rock.

Atmospheric pressure: The pressure exerted by the weight of air over a given area of Earth's surface.

Atoll: A ring-shaped collection of coral reefs that nearly or entirely enclose a lagoon.

B

Back reef: The landward side of a reef between the reefcrest and the land.

Backshore zone: The area of a beach normally affected by waves only during a storm at high tide.

Backswamp: The lower, poorly drained area of a floodplain that retains water.

Backwash: The return flow of water to the ocean following the swash of a wave.

Bajada: Several alluvial fans that have joined together.

Bar: A ridge or mound of sand or gravel that lies underwater a short distance from and parallel to a beach; also commonly known as a sand bar.

Barrier island: A bar that has been built up so that it rises above the normal high tide level.

Barrier reef: A long, narrow ridge of coral relatively near and parallel to a shoreline, separated from it by a lagoon.

Basal sliding: The sliding of a glacier over the ground on a layer of water.

Basalt: A dark, dense volcanic rock, about 50 percent of which is silica.

Base level: The level below which a stream cannot erode.

Basin: A hollow or depression in Earth's surface with no outlet for water.

Bay: A body of water in a curved inlet between headlands.

Beach: A deposit of loose material on shores that is moved by waves, tides, and, sometimes, winds.

Beach drift: The downwind movement of sand along a beach as a result of the zigzag pattern created by swash and backwash.

Bed load: The coarse sediment rolled along the bottom of a river or stream.

Bedrock: The general term for the solid rock that underlies the soil.

Berm: A distinct mound of sand or gravel running parallel to the shoreline that divides the foreshore zone from the backshore zone of a beach.

Blowout: A depression or low spot made in sand or light soil by strong wind.

Bottomset bed: A fine, horizontal layer of clay and silt deposited beyond the edge of a delta.

Breccia: A coarse-grained rock composed of angular, broken rock fragments held together by a mineral cement.

Butte: A flat-topped hill with steep sides that is smaller in area than a mesa.

C

Caldera: Large, usually circular, steep-walled basin at the summit of a volcano.

Canyon: A narrow, deep, rocky, and steep-walled valley carved by a swift-moving river.

Cap rock: Erosion-resistant rock that overlies other layers of less-resistant rock.

Cave: A naturally formed cavity or hollow beneath the surface of Earth that is beyond the zone of light and is large enough to be entered by humans.

Cavern: A large chamber within a cave.

Cave system: A series of caves connected by passages.

Channel: The depression where a stream flows or may flow.

Chemical weathering: The process by which chemical reactions alter the chemical makeup of rocks and minerals.

Cirque: A bowl-shaped depression carved out of a mountain by an alpine glacier.

Cliff: A high, steep face of rock.

Coast: A strip of land that extends landward from the coastline to the first major change in terrain features.

Coastal plain: A low, generally broad plain that lies between an oceanic shore and a higher landform such as a plateau or a mountain range.

Coastline: The boundary between the coast and the shore.

Comet: An icy extraterrestrial object that glows when it approaches the Sun, producing a long, wispy tail that points away from the Sun.

Compression: The reduction in the mass or volume of something by applying pressure.

Continental drift: The hypothesis proposed by Alfred Wegener that the continents are not stationary, but have moved across the surface of Earth over time.

Continental glacier: A glacier that forms over large areas of continents close to the poles.

Continental margin: The submerged outer edge of a continent, composed of the continental shelf and the continental slope.

Continental rise: The gently sloping, smooth-surfaced, thick accumulation of sediment at the base of certain continental slopes.

Continental shelf: The gently sloping region of the continental margin that extends seaward from the shoreline to the continental shelf break.

Continental shelf break: The outer edge of the continental shelf at which there is a sharp drop-off to the steeper continental slope.

Continental slope: The steeply sloping region of the continental margin that extends from the continental shelf break downward to the ocean basin.

Convection current: The circular movement of a gas or liquid between hot and cold areas.

Coral polyp: A small, invertebrate marine animal with tentacles that lives within a hard, cuplike skeleton that it secretes around itself.

Coral reef: A wave-resistant limestone structure produced by living organisms, found principally in shallow, tropical marine waters.

Cordillera: A complex group of mountain ranges, systems, and chains.

Creep: The extremely slow, almost continuous movement of soil and other material downslope.

Crest: The highest point or level; summit.

Crevasse: A deep, nearly vertical crack that develops in the upper portion of glacier ice.

Crust: The thin, solid outermost layer of Earth.

Curtain: A thin, wavy or folded sheetlike mineral deposit that hangs from the ceiling of a cave.

Cut bank: A steep, bare slope formed on the outside of a meander.

D

Debris avalanche: The extremely rapid downward movement of rocks, soil, mud, and other debris mixed with air and water.

Debris flow: A mixture of water and clay, silt, sand, and rock fragments that flows rapidly down steep slopes.

Deflation: The lowering of the land surface due to the removal of fine-grained particles by the wind.

Delta: A body of sediment deposited at the mouth of a river or stream where it enters an ocean or lake.

Desert pavement: Surface of flat desert lands covered with a layer of closely packed coarse pebbles and gravel.

Dip: The measured angle from the horizontal plane (Earth's surface) to a fault plane or bed of rock.

Dissolved load: Dissolved substances, the result of the chemical weathering of rock, that are carried along in a river or stream.

Distributaries: The channels that branch off of the main river in a delta, carrying water and sediment to the delta's edges.

Dune: A mound or ridge of loose, wind-blown sand.

E

Earthflow: The downward movement of water-saturated, clay-rich soil on a moderate slope.

Ecosystem: A system formed by the interaction of a community of plants, animals, and microorganisms with their environment.

Ejecta blanket: The circular layer of rock and dust lying immediately around a meteorite crater.

Emergent coast: A coast in which land formerly under water has gradually risen above sea level through geologic uplift of the land or has been exposed because of a drop in sea level.

Eolian: Formed or deposited by the action of the wind.

Erg: A vast area deeply covered with sand and topped with dunes.

Erosion: The gradual wearing away of Earth surfaces through the action of wind and water.

Erratic: A large boulder that a glacier deposits on a surface made of different rock.

Esker: A long, snakelike ridge of sediment deposited by a stream that ran under or within a glacier.

F

Fall: A sudden, steep drop of rock fragments or debris.

Fall line: The imaginary line that marks the sharp upward slope of land along a coastal plain's inland edge where waterfalls and rapids occur as rivers cross the zone from harder to softer rocks.

Fault: A crack or fracture in Earth's crust along which rock on one side has moved relative to rock on the other.

Fault creep: The slow, continuous movement of crustal blocks along a fault.

Fault line: The line on Earth's surface defining a fault; also known as a fault trace.

Fault plane: The area where crustal blocks meet and move along a fault from the fault line down into the crust.

Fault scarp: A steep-sided ledge or cliff generated as a result of fault movement.

Fault system: A network of connected faults.

Flash flood: A flood that occurs after a period of heavy rain, usually within six hours of the rain event.

Firn: The granular ice formed by the recrystallization of snow; also known as névé.

Fjord: A deep glacial trough submerged with seawater.

Floodplain: An area of nearly flat land bordering a stream or river that is naturally subject to periodic flooding.

Flow: A type of mass wasting that occurs when a loose mixture of debris, water, and air moves down a slope in a fluidlike manner.

Flowstone: The general term for a sheetlike mineral deposit on a wall or floor of a cave.

Fold: A bend or warp in a layered rock.

Foothill: A high hill at the base of a mountain.

Footwall: The crustal block that lies beneath an inclined fault plane.

Fore reef: The seaward edge of a reef that is fairly steep and slopes down to deeper water.

Foreset bed: An inclined layer of sand and gravel deposited along the edge of a delta.

Foreshore zone: The area of a beach between the ordinary low tide mark and the high tide mark.

Fracture zone: The area where faults occur at right angles to a main feature, such as a mid-ocean ridge.

Fringing reef: A coral reef formed close to a shoreline.

Fumarole: A small hole or vent in Earth's surface through which volcanic gases escape from underground.

G

Geyser: A hot spring that periodically erupts through an opening in Earth's surface, spewing hot water and steam.

Geyserite: A white or grayish silica-based deposit formed around hot springs.

Glacial drift: A general term for all material transported and deposited directly by or from glacial ice.

Glacial polish: The smooth and shiny surfaces produced on rocks underneath a glacier by material carried in the base of that glacier.

Glacial surge: The rapid forward movement of a glacier.

Glacial trough: A U-shaped valley carved out of a V-shaped stream valley by a valley glacier.

Glaciation: The transformation of the landscape through the action of glaciers.

Glacier: A large body of ice that formed on land by the compaction and recrystallization of snow, survives year to year, and shows some sign of movement downhill due to gravity.

Graben: A block of Earth's crust dropped downward between faults.

Graded stream: A stream that is maintaining a balance between the processes of erosion and deposition.

Granular flow: A flow that contains up to 20 percent water.

Gravity: The physical force of attraction between any two objects in the universe.

Ground moraine: A continuous layer of till deposited beneath a steadily retreating glacier.

Groundwater: Freshwater lying within the uppermost parts of Earth's crust, filling the pore spaces in soil and fractured rock.

Gully: A channel cut into Earth's surface by running water, especially after a heavy rain.

Guyot: An undersea, flat-topped seamount.

H

Hanging valley: A shallow glacial trough that leads into the side of a larger, main glacial trough.

Hanging wall: The crustal block that lies above an inclined fault plane.

Headland: An elevated area of hard rock that projects out into an ocean or other large body of water.

Hill: A highland that rises up to 1,000 feet (305 meters) above its surroundings, has a rounded top, and is less rugged in outline than a mountain.

Horn: A high mountain peak that forms when the walls of three or more glacial cirques intersect.

Horst: A block of Earth's crust forced upward between faults.

Hot spot: An area beneath Earth's crust where magma currents rise.

Hot spring: A pool of hot water that has seeped through an opening in Earth's surface.

I

Igneous rock: Rock formed by the cooling and hardening of magma, molten rock that is underground (called lava once it reaches Earth's surface).

Internal flow: The movement of ice inside a glacier through the deformation and realignment of ice crystals; also known as creep.

Invertebrates: Animals without backbones.

K

Kame: A steep-sided, conical mound or hill formed of glacial drift that is created when sediment is washed into a depression on the top surface of a glacier and is then deposited on the ground below when the glacier melts away.

Karst topography: A landscape characterized by the presence of sinkholes, caves, springs, and losing streams.

Kettle: A shallow, bowl-shaped depression formed when a large block of glacial ice breaks away from the main glacier and is buried beneath glacial till, then melts. If the depression fills with water, it is known as a kettle lake.

L

Lagoon: A quiet, shallow stretch of water separated from the open sea by an offshore reef or other type of landform.

Lahar: A mudflow composed of volcanic ash, rocks, and water produced by a volcanic eruption.

Landslide: A general term used to describe all relatively rapid forms of mass wasting.

Lateral moraine: A moraine deposited along the side of a valley glacier.

Lava: Magma that has reached Earth's surface.

Lava dome: Mass of lava, created by many individual flows, that forms in the crater of a volcano after a major eruption.

Leeward: On or toward the side facing away from the wind.

Levee (natural): A low ridge or mound along a stream bank, formed by deposits left when floodwater slows down on leaving the channel.

Limestone: A sedimentary rock composed primarily of the mineral calcite (calcium carbonate).

Lithosphere: The rigid uppermost section of the mantle combined with the crust.

Longshore current: An ocean current that flows close and almost parallel to the shoreline and is caused by the angled rush of waves toward the shore.

Longshore drift: The movement of sand and other material along a shoreline in the longshore current.

Losing stream: A stream on Earth's surface that is diverted underground through a sinkhole or a cave.

M

Magma: Molten rock containing particles of mineral grains and dissolved gas that forms deep within Earth.

Magma chamber: A reservoir or cavity beneath Earth's surface containing magma that feeds a volcano.

Mantle: The thick, dense layer of rock that lies beneath Earth's crust.

Mass wasting: The spontaneous movement of material down a slope in response to gravity.

Meander: A bend or loop in a stream's course.

Mechanical weathering: The process by which a rock or mineral is broken down into smaller fragments without altering its chemical makeup.

Medial moraine: A moraine formed when two adjacent glaciers flow into each other and their lateral moraines are caught in the middle of the joined glacier.

Meltwater: The water from melted snow or ice.

Mesa: A flat-topped hill or mountain with steep sides that is smaller in area than a plateau.

Metamorphic rock: Rock whose texture or composition has been changed by extreme heat and pressure.

Meteor: A glowing fragment of extraterrestrial material passing through Earth's atmosphere.

Meteorite: A fragment of extraterrestrial material that strikes the surface of Earth.

Meteorite crater: A crater or depression in the surface of a celestial body caused by the impact of a meteorite; also known as an impact crater.

Meteoroid: A small, solid body floating in space.

Mid-ocean ridge: A long, continuous volcanic mountain range found on the basins of all oceans.

Moraine: The general term for a ridge or mound of till deposited by a glacier.

Mountain: A landmass that rises 1,000 feet (305 meters) or more above its surroundings and has steep sides meeting in a summit that is much narrower in width than the base of the landmass.

Mudflow: A mixture primarily of the smallest silt and clay particles and water that has the consistency of newly mixed concrete and flows quickly down slopes.

Mud pot: A hot spring that contains thick, muddy clay.

O

Oasis: A fertile area in a desert or other dry region where groundwater reaches the surface through springs or wells.

Ocean basin: That part of Earth's surface that extends seaward from a continental margin.

Oxbow lake: A crescent-shaped body of water formed from a single loop that was cut off from a meandering stream.

P

Paleomagnetism: The study of changes in the intensity and direction of Earth's magnetic field through time.

Passive continental margin: A continental margin that has a broad continental shelf, a gentle continental slope, and a pronounced continental rise; it is marked by a lack of earthquake and volcanic activity.

Peneplain: A broad, low, almost featureless surface allegedly created by long-continued erosion.

Photosynthesis: The process by which plants use energy from sunlight to change water and carbon dioxide into sugars and starches.

Piedmont glacier: A valley glacier that flows out of a mountainous area onto a gentle slope or plain and spreads out over the surrounding terrain.

Pinnacle: A tall, slender tower or spire of rock.

Plateau: A relatively level, large expanse of land that rises some 1,500 feet (457 meters) or more above its surroundings and has at least one steep side.

Plates: Large sections of Earth's lithosphere separated by deep fault zones.

Plate tectonics: The geologic theory that Earth's crust is composed of rigid plates that "float" toward or away from each other, either directly or indirectly, shifting continents, forming mountains and new ocean crust, and stimulating volcanic eruptions.

Playa: A shallow, short-lived lake that forms where water drains into a basin and quickly evaporates, leaving a flat surface of clay, silt, and minerals.

Point bar: The low, crescent-shaped deposit of sediment on the inside of a meander.

Pyroclastic material: Rock fragments, crystals, ash, pumice, and glass shards formed by a volcanic explosion or ejection from a volcanic vent.

R

Rapids: The section of a stream where water flows fast over hard rocks.

Reef crest: The high point of a coral reef that is almost always exposed at low tide.

Regolith: The layer of loose, uncemented rocks and rock fragments of various size that lies beneath the soil and above the bedrock.

Rhyolite: A fine-grained type of volcanic rock that has a high silica content.

Rift valley: The deep central crevice in a mid-ocean ridge; also, a valley or trough formed between two normal faults.

Ring of Fire: The name given to the geographically active belt around the Pacific Ocean that is home to more than 75 percent of the planet's volcanoes.

River: A large stream.

Rock flour: Fine-grained rock material produced when a glacier abrades or scrapes rock beneath it.

S

Saltation: The jumping movement of sand caused by the wind.

Sea arch: An arch created by the erosion of weak rock in a sea cliff through wave action.

Seafloor spreading: The process by which new oceanic crust is formed by the upwelling of magma at mid-ocean ridges, resulting in the continuous lateral movement of existing oceanic crust.

Seamount: An isolated volcanic mountain that often rises 3,280 feet (1,000 meters) or more above the surrounding ocean floor.

Sea stack: An isolated column of rock, the eroded remnant of a sea arch, located in the ocean a short distance from the shoreline.

Sediment: Rock debris such as gravel, sand, silt, and clay.

Sedimentary rock: Rock that is formed by the accumulation and compression of sediment, which may consist of rock fragments, remains of microscopic organisms, and minerals.

Shear stress: The force of gravity acting on an object on a slope, pulling it downward in a direction parallel to the slope.

Shock wave: Wave of increased temperature and pressure formed by the sudden compression of the medium through which the wave moves.

Shore: The strip of ground bordering a body of water that is alternately covered or exposed by waves or tides.

Shoreline: The fluctuating line between water and the shore.

Silica: An oxide (a compound of an element and oxygen) found in magma that, when cooled, crystallizes to become the mineral quartz, which is one of the most common compounds found in Earth's crust.

Silt: Fine earthy particles smaller than sand carried by moving water and deposited as a sediment.

Sinkhole: A bowl-like depression that develops on Earth's surface above a cave ceiling that has collapsed or on an area where the underlying sedimentary rock has been eroded away.

Slide: The movement of a mass of rocks or debris down a slope.

Slip face: The steeply sloped side of a dune that faces away from the wind.

Slope failure: A type of mass wasting that occurs when debris moves downward as the result of a sudden failure on a steep slope or cliff.

Slump: The downward movement of blocks of material on a curved surface.

Slurry flow: A flow that contains between 20 and 40 percent water.

Snow line: The elevation above which snow can form and remain all year.

Solifluction: A form of mass wasting that occurs in relatively cold regions in which waterlogged soil flows very slowly down a slope.

Speleothem: A mineral deposit formed in a cave.

Spit: A long, narrow deposit of sand or gravel that projects from land into open water.

Stalactite: An icicle-shaped mineral deposit hanging from the roof of a cave.

Stalagmite: A cone-shaped mineral deposit projecting upward from the floor of a cave.

Strain: The change in a rock's shape or volume (or both) in response to stress.

Strata: The layers in a series of sedimentary rocks.

Stream: Any body of running water that moves downslope under the influence of gravity in a narrow and defined channel on Earth's surface.

Stress: The force acting on an object (per unit of area).

Striations: The long, parallel scratches and grooves produced in rocks underneath a glacier as it moves over them.

Strike: The compass direction of a fault line.

Subduction zone: A region where two plates come together and the edge of one plate slides beneath the other.

Submarine canyon: A steep-walled, V-shaped canyon that is cut into the rocks and sediments of the continental slope and, sometimes, the outer continental shelf.

Submergent coast: A coast in which formerly dry land has been gradually flooded, either by land sinking or by sea level rising.

Surface creep: The rolling and pushing of sand and slightly larger particles by the wind.

Suspended load: The fine-grained sediment that is suspended in the flow of water in a river or stream.

Swash: The rush of water up the shore after the breaking of a wave.

Symbiosis: The close, long-term association between two organisms of different species, which may or may not be beneficial for both organisms.

Syncline: A downward-curving (concave) fold in rock that resembles a trough.

T

Talus: A sloping pile of rock fragments lying at the base of the cliff or steep slope from which they have broken off; also known as scree.

Tarn: A small lake that fills the central depression in a cirque.

Terminal moraine: A moraine found near the terminus of a glacier; also known as an end moraine.

Terminus: The leading edge of a glacier; also known as the glacier snout.

Terrace: The exposed portion of a former floodplain that stands like a flat bench above the outer edges of the new floodplain.

Tide: The periodic rising and falling of water in oceans and other large bodies of water that results from the gravitational attraction of the Moon and the Sun upon Earth.

Till: A random mixture of finely crushed rock, sand, pebbles, and boulders deposited by a glacier.

Tombolo: A mound of sand or other beach material that rises above the water to connect an offshore island to the shore or to another island.

Topset bed: A horizontal layer of coarse sand and gravel deposited on top of a delta.

Travertine: A dense, white deposit formed from calcium carbonate that creates rock formations around hot springs.

Trench: A long, deep, narrow depression on the ocean basin with relatively steep sides.

Turbidity current: A turbulent mixture of water and sediment that flows down a continental slope under the influence of gravity.

U

Uplift: In geology, the slow upward movement of large parts of stable areas of Earth's crust.

U-shaped valley: A valley created by glacial erosion that has a profile suggesting the form of the letter "U," characterized by steep sides that may curve inwards at their base and a broad, nearly flat floor.

V

Valley glacier: An alpine glacier flowing downward through a preexisting stream valley.

Ventifact: A stone or bedrock surface that has been shaped or eroded by the wind.

Viscosity: The measure of a fluid's resistance to flow.

Volcano: A vent or hole in Earth's surface through which magma, hot gases, ash, and rock fragments escape from deep inside the planet; the term is also used to describe the cone of erupted material that builds up around that opening.

V-shaped valley: A narrow valley created by the downcutting action of a stream that has a profile suggesting the form of the letter "V," characterized by steeply sloping sides.

W

Waterfall: An often steep drop in a stream bed causing the water in a stream channel to fall vertically or nearly vertically.

Wave crest: The highest part of a wave.

Wave-cut notch: An indentation produced by wave erosion at the base of a sea cliff.

Wave-cut platform: A horizontal bench of rock formed beneath the waves at the base of a sea cliff as it retreats because of wave erosion.

Wave height: The vertical distance between the wave crest and the wave trough.

Wavelength: The horizontal distance between two wave crests or troughs.

Wave trough: The lowest part of a wave form between two crests.

Weathering: The process by which rocks and minerals are broken down at or near Earth's surface.

Windward: On or toward the side facing into the wind.

Y

Yardang: Wind-sculpted, streamlined ridge that lies parallel to the prevailing winds.

Yazoo stream: A small stream that enters a floodplain and flows alongside a larger stream or river for quite a distance before eventually flowing into the larger waterway.

Z

Zooxanthellae: Microscopic algae that live symbiotically within the cells of some marine invertebrates, especially coral.

Ocean basin

The features of continental landscapes are mirrored by similar features on the ocean basins. Plateaus, plains, valleys, rolling hills, and volcanic cones and mountains are found beneath the waters of the oceans, just as they are on dry land. Yet the largest underwater mountains are higher than those on the continents, and underwater plains are flatter and more extensive than their dry counterparts. These "oceanscapes," at one time unseen and unknown, may resemble familiar landscapes, but on a much grander scale.

The shape of the land

Ocean basins are that part of Earth's surface that extends seaward from the continental margins (the submerged outer edges of continents, each composed of a continental shelf and a continental slope). Basins lie at an average water depth of about 12,450 feet (3,795 meters). From there they drop steeply down into the deepest trenches. The oceans and seas of the planet form a layer of water that covers approximately 71 percent of Earth's surface. Ocean basins occupy more than 76 percent of the total ocean area.

Many sources include the continental margins as part of the ocean basins, but the margins are the drowned edges of the continents. They are part of the same crust (thin, solid outermost layer of Earth) that forms the continents. The transition between continental crust and oceanic crust occurs in the continental slope. Continental crust is composed mostly of granite, whereas oceanic crust is mostly basalt. Although they differ in composition, both are types of igneous rock that forms when magma cools and solidifies. Granite forms when magma with a high silica content cools slowly deep beneath Earth's surface; basalt forms when magma with a low silica content cools quickly outside of or very near Earth's surface. (For

Canning Basin, western Australia. Ocean basins are that part of Earth's surface that extends seaward from the continental margins. PHOTOGRAPH REPRODUCED BY PERMISSION OF THE CORBIS CORPORATION.

further information on continental margins, see the **Continental margin** chapter.)

By ocean basins, this discussion is referring to what may be termed the deep-ocean basins: those areas of the ocean floor lying more than 10,500 feet (3,200 meters) beneath the surface of the oceans. The four main ocean basins are those of the Pacific, Atlantic, Indian, and Arctic Oceans. The Pacific Ocean, which occupies about one-third of Earth's surface, has the largest basin. Its basin also has the greatest average depth at approximately 14,000 feet (4,300 meters). The Atlantic Ocean basin is half the size of that of the Pacific Ocean and is not quite as deep, averaging about 12,000 feet (3,660 meters). While slightly smaller in size than the Atlantic Ocean basin, the Indian Ocean basin sits at a lower average depth, 12,750 feet (3,885 meters). The Arctic Ocean basin is less than 10 percent the size of the Pacific Ocean basin and lies at an average depth of 3,900 feet (1,190 meters).

All ocean basins contain certain primary features: mid-ocean ridges, abyssal (pronounced ah-BISS-ul) plains, trenches, and seamounts.

Perhaps the most impressive features found on all ocean basins are long, continuous volcanic mountain ranges called mid-ocean ridges. These elevated ridges mark the area where sections of oceanic crust are pulling apart from each other. As they do, hot magma (liquid rock) emerges from beneath the crust and seeps forth as lava to fill the crack continuously created by the separation. The lava cools and attaches to the trailing edge of each section, forming new ocean floor crust in a process known as seafloor spreading. Additional lava is deposited by the thousands of volcanoes that periodically erupt along the ridges.

The large depression that is created between the spreading sections is known as a rift valley. Mid-ocean ridges are divided into three groups depending on their spreading rates: slow, medium, and fast. Ridges that spread slowly, from 0.4 to 2 inches (1 to 5 centimeters) per year, have a wide and deep central rift valley. The valley may be 6 miles (10 kilometers) wide and 2 miles (3 kilometers) deep below the crests, or tops, of the ridges that surround it on either side. Ridges that are classified as medium spread at a rate of 2 to 4 inches (5 to 10 centimeters) per year. The valleys of these ridges may be up to 3 miles (5 kilometers) across and range in depth from 165 to 655 feet (50 to 200 meters). Finally, fast-spreading ridges open up at a rate of 4 to 8 inches (10 to 20 centimeters) per year. Their rift valleys are much smoother in appearance. On average, these small valleys are only 330 feet (100 meters) wide and 33 to 66 feet (10 to 20 meters) deep.

In most locations, mid-ocean ridges are 6,500 feet (1,980 meters) or more below the surface of the oceans. In a few places, however, they actually extend above sea level and form islands. Iceland (in the North Atlantic), the Azores (west of the coast of Portugal), and Tristan de Cunha (in the south Atlantic midway between southern Africa and South America) are examples of such islands.

The most-studied mid-ocean ridge in the world is the Mid-Atlantic Ridge. It begins at the tip of Greenland and runs down the center of the Atlantic Ocean between the Americas on the west and Europe and Africa on the east. It ends its course at the southern tip of the African continent. At that point, the ridge continues around the eastern edge of Africa as the Southwest Indian Ridge. That ridge then divides near the center of the Indian Ocean basin into the Central Indian Ridge that runs north into the African continent and the Southeast Indian Ridge that runs east below the Australian continent. The ridge continues eastward along the southern portion of the Pacific Ocean basin as the Pacific Antarctic Ridge. It eventually heads northward along the western coastline of South and Central America as the East Pacific Rise.

These mid-ocean ridges combine to form a global undersea mountain system known as the mid-ocean ridge system. Extending more than 40,000 miles (64,000 kilometers), it is the longest topographic or surface feature on Earth. Snaking its way between the continents, the ridge system encircles the planet like the seams on a baseball. Whereas the seams form a continuous loop, the mid-ocean ridge system is offset in many places. The offsets are called fracture zones. These breaks in the ridge line are caused by faults, cracks or fractures in Earth's crust along which rock on one side has moved relative to rock on the other. Ocean crust on either side of a fault in a fracture zone slides in opposite directions. This helps relieve tension created when different sections of a mid-ocean ridge spread at different rates. The faults form deep, linear gouges almost perpendicular to the ridges. Crust in a fracture zone looks like it has been sliced up by a giant knife. The largest fracture zone occurs along the Mid-Atlantic Ridge, offsetting it by 590 miles (950 kilometers).

The relatively flat areas of ocean basins between continental margins and mid-ocean ridges are called abyssal plains. They are generally found at depths of 13,000 to 16,000 feet (3,960 to 4,875 meters). Likely the most level places on Earth, they are far flatter than any plain on dry land. They have gentle slopes of less than 1 foot (0.3 meter) of elevation difference for each 1,000 feet (305 meters) of distance.

The flatness of abyssal plains is due to an accumulation of layers of sediments formed from the remains of marine life and rock debris such as gravel, sand, silt, and clay. Much of this rock debris has been washed off the surface of the continents for hundreds of thousands of years. It is carried down continental slopes by turbidity currents, turbulent mixtures of water and sediment. Pulled by gravity, these currents may surge downward like an avalanche at up to 50 miles (80 kilometers) per hour. When the currents reach the ocean basin, they slow and the sediment they carry falls on the abyssal plains. In many areas, these sediment layers measure up to 3 miles (5 kilometers) thick. The sediments cover many of the irregularities that may exist in the basaltic rock of the ocean floor. In places where the layers of sediment are thinner, gently sloping hills may rise from the abyssal plains to heights less than 3,280 feet (1,000 meters). Known as abyssal hills, these low, oval-shaped hills are typically volcanic in origin.

The deepest parts of ocean basins are trenches, which may descend over 36,000 feet (11,000 meters) beneath the surface of an ocean. These long, narrow, canyonlike structures are formed where sections of oceanic crust are moving and sliding under sections of continental crust. Thus, trenches are often found parallel to continental margins and the seaward

Words to Know

Abyssal hill: A gently sloping, small hill, typically of volcanic origin, found on an abyssal plain.

Abyssal plain: The relatively flat area of an ocean basin between a continental margin and a mid-ocean ridge.

Asthenosphere: The section of the mantle immediately beneath the lithosphere that is composed of partially melted rock.

Continental drift: The hypothesis proposed by Alfred Wegener that the continents are not stationary, but have moved across the surface of Earth over time.

Continental margin: The submerged outer edge of a continent, composed of the continental shelf and the continental slope.

Convection current: The circular movement of a gas or liquid between hot and cold areas.

Crust: The thin, solid outermost layer of Earth.

Fault: A crack or fracture in Earth's crust along which rock on one side has moved relative to rock on the other.

Fracture zone: An area where faults occur at right angles to a main feature, such as a mid-ocean ridge.

Guyot: An undersea, flat-topped seamount.

Hot spot: An area beneath Earth's crust where magma currents rise.

Lithosphere: The rigid uppermost section of the mantle combined with the crust.

Mantle: The thick, dense layer of rock that lies beneath Earth's crust.

Mid-ocean ridge: A long, continuous volcanic mountain range found on the basins of all oceans.

Paleomagnetism: The study of changes in the intensity and direction of Earth's magnetic field through time.

Plates: Large sections of Earth's lithosphere that are separated by deep fault zones.

Plate tectonics: The geologic theory that Earth's crust is composed of rigid plates that "float" toward or away from each other, either directly or indirectly, shifting continents, forming mountains and new ocean crust, and stimulating volcanic eruptions.

Rift valley: The deep central crevice in a mid-ocean ridge; also, a valley or trough formed between two normal faults.

Seafloor spreading: The process by which new oceanic crust is formed by the upwelling of magma at mid-ocean ridges, resulting in the continuous lateral movement of existing oceanic crust.

Seamount: An isolated volcanic mountain that often rises 3,280 feet (1,000 meters) or more above the surrounding ocean floor.

Subduction zone: A region where two plates come together and the edge of one plate slides beneath the other.

Trench: A long, deep, narrow depression on the ocean basin with relatively steep sides.

Turbidity current: A turbulent mixture of water and sediment that flows down a continental slope under the influence of gravity.

edge of volcanic island arcs like Japan, the Philippines, and the Aleutian Islands. Of the twenty-two trenches that have been identified around the world, eighteen are located in the Pacific Ocean basin, three in the Atlantic Ocean basin, and one in the Indian Ocean basin.

Glomar Challenger

In 1968, the oceanographic drilling and coring vessel *Glomar Challenger* was launched on a voyage to study the geological evolution of Earth. From its platform, it was possible to lower up to 20,000 feet (6,096 meters) of pipe into the open ocean, bore into the seafloor to a depth of 2,500 feet (762 meters), and then bring up samples (or cores) of the crust beneath the ocean.

During her fifteen years of operation, the *Glomar Challenger* operated in all the major oceans and seas of the world. For the geologic community, each of her voyages was the equivalent of a moon shot. The core samples the vessel retrieved were from a remote and largely unexplored portion of Earth's surface. From those samples, geologists were able to establish that Alfred Wegener's hypothesis of continental drift was correct. They were also able to prove the theory of seafloor spreading and determine that the oldest oceanic crust was far younger than the oldest continental crust. From samples taken during later voyages, geologists were able to prove that Earth's magnetic poles have reversed themselves over time.

Seamounts are isolated volcanic mountains that often rise 3,280 feet (1,000 meters) or more above the surrounding ocean floor. Sometimes seamounts rise above sea level to create islands. Geologists estimate that there may be as many as 85 million seamounts on the floors of the world's oceans. Seamounts usually form near mid-ocean ridges or above hot spots, areas where magma plumes melt through Earth's crust to form volcanoes. Hot spot plumes may exist for millions of years. As a section of oceanic crust moves over the hot spot, a chain of volcanoes may be produced. The Hawaiian Islands are an example of such activity.

When volcanic activity ceases, a seamount begins to erode and collapse back into an ocean. If wave action and weathering continue long enough while the seamount is still above sea level, its top may be eroded flat. An undersea, flat-topped seamount is called a guyot (pronounced GHEE-oh). These types of seamounts are common in the western Pacific Ocean.

Forces and changes: Construction and destruction

Prior to World War II (1939–45), the floors of the oceans had been a part of Earth that had received little scientific study. During the war, the U.S. military employed geologists to carry out studies of the sea floors to find hiding places that might be used by both friendly and enemy submarines. The studies, which involved measuring the depth of ocean floors, revealed two important surface features on the floors: mid-ocean ridges and trenches. The geologists also made another important discovery. While using an underwater instrument that measured magnetic materials in order to detect submarines, they found alternating magnetic differences on the ocean floors.

Scientists believe the magnetic field that exists around the planet is generated by Earth's core. The very center of the planet, Earth's core begins some 1,800 miles (2,900 kilometers) beneath the planet's surface and extends to a depth of 3,960 miles (6,370 kilometers). Composed of the metal elements iron and nickel, the core has a solid inner portion and a liquid outer portion. As Earth rotates, so does that iron-bearing core, creating the magnetic field that may be detected with a compass.

Puzzled by the magnetic anomalies found on the ocean floors, geologists in the 1950s began to explore the possible reasons through the study of paleomagnetism (pronounced pay-lee-oh-MAG-nuh-ti-zum; the study of changes in the intensity and direction of Earth's magnetic field through geologic time). They discovered that almost all rocks contain some type of magnetic material. After a rock has formed and begins to cool, the grain or grains of magnetic material in the rock become aligned with the polarity (north-south directionality) of Earth's magnetic field at that time. In effect, a permanent record of Earth's magnetic field at the time the rock cooled and solidified is locked into its magnetic grains.

Studying the magnetic properties of rocks from different locations around the planet, geologists found that Earth's magnetic poles appeared to have wandered around the globe for at least the past several million years. Since this seemed unlikely, geologists concluded that the continents themselves must have moved across the surface of the planet, carrying the magnetic rocks with them. This brought new attention to the hypothesis of continental drift. (A hypothesis is an educated guess, while a theory is a principle supported by extensive scientific evidence and testing.)

Continental drift

In 1910, German geophysicist Alfred Wegener (1880–1930) had begun arguing that Earth's continents do not remain in a fixed position on the planet's surface. He believed instead that they are mobile and over vast amounts of time have drifted across the surface. Wegener called his hypothesis continental drift. He based his hypothesis on the idea that the coastlines of several of the world's continents fit remarkably together. From this, he proposed that the continents had once been joined together in one large continental mass. He called this supercontinent Pangaea (pronounced pan-JEE-ah; from the Greek words meaning "all lands"). What Wegener lacked, however, was a convincing explanation as to what moved the continents along the surface.

Seafloor spreading is the theory that explains how the floors of oceans had split apart and rocks on either side of the ridges are moving away from each other.

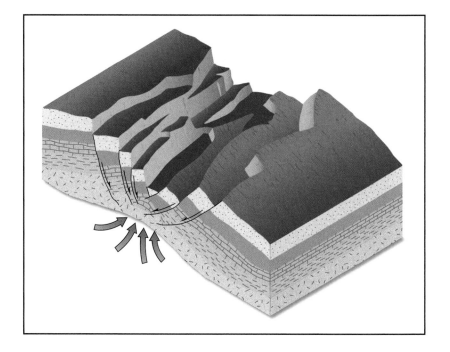

Seafloor spreading

A little more than fifty years after Wegener first proposed his hypothesis, American geologist Harry H. Hess (1906–69) offered up his own hypothesis: seafloor spreading. Hess proposed that mid-ocean ridges were areas where the floors of oceans had split apart and where rocks on either side of the ridges were moving away from each other. At the center of the ridges, lava from below welled up and solidified into new volcanic rock on the ocean floors. Like a giant conveyer belt, the spreading ocean floor carried rock away from the ridges in either direction. The youngest rocks were located along the ridges where new lava rose up. The farther the rocks had moved from the ridges, the older they were.

Within a few years of Hess's proposal, geologists discovered that over short time scales, Earth's magnetic field undergoes polarity reversals (the north magnetic pole becomes the south magnetic pole and vice versa). Although not entirely sure of the reasons, geologists know this occurs every 500,000 years or so. As these magnetic reversals occurred in the past, the changing polarities—normal, reversed, normal, reversed—were recorded in newly forming rocks along mid-ocean ridges. When tied with the idea of seafloor spreading, this helped explain the magnetic differences geologists had found on the ocean floors during World War II.

Combining continental drift and seafloor spreading, geologists were able to develop a unifying theory that helped explain how landforms and other geologic features are created and how Earth's surface changes over time. That revolutionary theory is known as plate tectonics.

Plate tectonics

The processes occurring in Earth, from the core to the crust, have put the surface of the planet in motion, constantly changing its shape. Geologists divide the surface and the interior of Earth into layers. As mentioned, the core is at the very center of the planet. Above the core is the mantle, which extends up to about 31 miles (50 kilometers) below the surface of the planet. The mantle accounts for approximately 80 percent of the volume of Earth. Above the mantle lies the brittle crust, the thin shell of rock that covers Earth.

The upper portion of the mantle is rigid. Geologists combine this section of the mantle with the overlying crust, calling it the lithosphere (pronounced LITH-uh-sfeer). The lithosphere measures roughly 60 miles (100 kilometers) thick. The part of the mantle immediately beneath the lithosphere is called the asthenosphere (pronounced as-THEN-uh-sfeer). This layer is composed of partially melted rock that has the consistency of putty and extends to a depth of about 155 miles (250 kilometers).

The lithosphere is broken into many pieces called tectonic or crustal plates, which vary in size and shape. They are in constant contact with each other, fitting together like pieces in a jigsaw puzzle. They float on the semi-molten asthenosphere, and because they are interconnected, no plate can move without affecting those around it. What causes the plates to move are convection currents, which originate at the base of the mantle where it surrounds the core.

With estimated temperatures in the core exceeding 9,900°F (5,482°C), tremendous heat energy is generated there. If that energy were not released in some manner, the interior of the planet would melt. This is prevented by the convection currents, which carry the energy to the surface of the planet where it is released.

Convection currents act similar to the currents produced in a pot of boiling liquid on a hot stove. When a liquid in a pot begins to boil, it turns over and over. Liquid heated at the bottom of the pot rises to the surface because heating has caused it to expand and become less dense (lighter). Once at the surface, the heated material cools and becomes dense once more. It then sinks back down to the bottom to become reheated. This continuous motion of heated material rising, cooling, and sinking forms the circular-moving convection currents.

Like an enormous stove, the core heats the mantle rock that immediately surrounds it. Expanding and becoming less dense, the heated rock slowly rises through cooler, denser mantle rock above it. When it reaches

Hydrothermal Vents

Hydrothermal vents are cracks in the ocean floor or chimneylike structures extending from the ocean floor generally up to 150 feet (45 meters) high. Some are much higher. They are usually found at mid-ocean ridges where volcanic activity is present. Using deep-sea submersible vessels, scientists first discovered hydrothermal vents in the Pacific Ocean in 1977.

These vents release hot mineral-laden water into the surrounding ocean. Temperature of this fluid is typically around 660°F (350°C). Because of the high pressure exerted by water at ocean floor depths, hydrothermal fluids can exceed 212°F (100°C) without boiling. Often, the fluid released is black due to the presence of very fine sulfide mineral particles that contain iron, copper, zinc, and other metals. As a result, these deep-ocean hot springs are called black smokers.

Hydrothermal vents are surrounded by unusual forms of sea life, including giant clams, tube worms, and unique types of fish. These organisms live off bacteria that thrive on the energy-rich chemical compounds transported by hydrothermal fluids. This is the only environment on Earth supported by a food chain that does not depend on the energy of the Sun or photosynthesis. The energy source is chemical, not solar, and is called chemosynthesis.

Hydrothermal vents in the Gulf of California's Guaymas Basin. **PHOTOGRAPH REPRODUCED BY PERMISSION OF THE CORBIS CORPORATION.**

the lithosphere, the heated rock moves along the base of the lithosphere, exerting dragging forces on the tectonic plates. This causes the plates to move. In the process, the heated rock begins to lose heat. Cooling and becoming denser, the rock then sinks back toward the core, where it will be heated once more. Scientists estimate that it takes mantle rock 200 million years to make the circular trip from the core to the lithosphere and back again.

On average, a plate inches its way across the surface of Earth at a rate no faster than human fingernails grow, which is roughly 2 inches (5 centimeters) per year. As it moves, a plate can transform or slide along another, converge or move into another, or diverge or move away from another. The boundaries where plates meet and interact are known as plate margins.

When two continental plates converge, they will crumple up and compress, forming complex mountain ranges. When an oceanic plate converges with a continental plate or another oceanic plate, it will sink beneath the other plate. This is because oceanic crust is made of basalt, which is denser (heavier) than the granite rocks that compose continental crust. The process of one tectonic plate sinking beneath another is known as subduction, and the region where it occurs is known as a subduction zone.

When a tectonic plate subducts beneath another, the leading edge of the subducting plate is pushed farther and farther beneath the surface. When it reaches about 70 miles (112 kilometers) into the mantle, high temperature and pressure melt the rock at the edge of the plate, forming thick, flowing magma. Since it is less dense than the rock that typically surrounds it deep underground, magma tends to rise toward Earth's surface, forcing its way through weakened layers of rock. Most often, magma collects in underground reservoirs called magma chambers where it remains until it is ejected onto the planet's surface through vents called volcanoes. (For further information, see the **Volcano** chapter.)

Mid-ocean ridges and diverging plates

A mid-ocean ridge is a plate margin where two tectonic plates are diverging. Molten rocks emerge from beneath the crest of the ridge. Geologists estimate that 75 percent of the molten rocks or magma reaching Earth's surface does so through mid-ocean ridges. Coming in contact with seawater, the magma solidifies, forming new ocean crust at the trailing ends of the diverging plates. Rocks solidifying at the ridge crest record the current polarity of Earth's magnetic field.

Fast-spreading ridges have more magma beneath them and more volcanic eruptions occur along the ridges. These ridges seem to spread

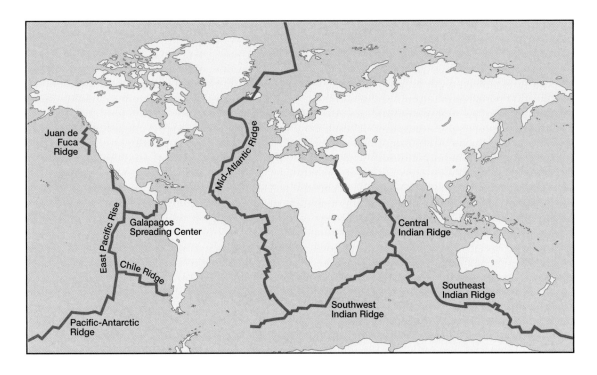

The system of mid-ocean ridges, or submarine volcanic mountain ranges, around the world. Geologists estimate that 75 percent of the molten rocks or magma reaching Earth's surface does so through mid-ocean ridges.

somewhat smoothly like hot taffy being pulled apart. Slower-spreading ridges have less magma, and the ocean crust in these areas cracks and breaks as it is pulled apart. The age of rocks in ocean basins increases the farther away they are from ridges. They are also more deeply buried by sediments because those sediments have had a longer time to collect.

Because Earth is in a constant dynamic state, creation and expansion of the crust in one area requires the destruction of the crust elsewhere. On the planet, new crust is formed at diverging plate margins and destroyed at subduction zones. Continental crust may be more than 3 billion years old, but oceanic crust is less than 200 million years old. The recycling of oceanic crust takes place between mid-ocean ridges (where it is created) and huge ocean trenches (where it is destroyed). The Pacific Ocean basin, containing the vast majority of the world's trenches, is currently shrinking as the other ocean basins are expanding.

In a subduction zone, an oceanic plate folds downward, plunging steeply under the adjacent plate and descending into the mantle where it is reabsorbed and returned to a molten state, beginning the cycle all over again. Part of that molten material may rise to the surface again through fractures in the crust. As a consequence, numerous volcanoes are formed parallel to the trenches on the side opposite to that of the subducting oceanic plate. Where the trenches are located in the ocean, as in the

Western Pacific, these volcanoes form arcs or chains of volcanic islands. Where the trenches run along the margins of continents, chains of volcanic mountains are formed near the edges of the continents, such as the Andes Mountains in South America.

Spotlight on famous forms

Loihi Seamount, Pacific Ocean

Loihi (pronounced low-EE-hee) is the youngest volcano associated with the Hawaiian Islands chain. It is located about 20 miles (32 kilometers) off the southeastern shore of the island of Hawaii. The basin-shaped summit of the volcano lies 3,178 feet (969 meters) below sea level.

Prior to 1970, geologists believed the seamount was inactive and similar to the other seamounts that surround the Hawaiian Islands. Many of these other seamounts are 80 to 100 million years old. Geologists soon discovered repeated, intense earthquake activity (called swarms) at Loihi. In 1996, the volcano erupted and has been intermittently active since then. If Loihi erupts at rates comparable to other active volcanoes in the Hawaiian Islands, geologists believe it will reach sea level in a few tens of thousands of years.

Mariana Trench, Pacific Ocean

The deepest point on the surface of Earth is found in the Mariana Trench, which is located in the basin of the Pacific Ocean southeast of the Mariana Islands. The trench marks the location where the Pacific Plate is subducting beneath the Philippine Plate. Measuring 1,580 miles (2,542 kilometers) long and 43 miles (69 kilometers) wide, the arc-shaped trench plunges to a maximum depth of 36,201 feet (11,034 meters). The pressure at that great depth is more than 16,000 pounds per square inch (1,125 kilograms per square centimeter). If Mount Everest, the highest point on land, were set into the trench at its deepest point, more than 7,000 feet (2,134 meters) of water would still cover the mountain's peak.

The trench's deepest point, located near its southern extremity, is called the Challenger Deep. It was named after *Challenger II,* the British naval research vessel that discovered it in 1951. In 1960, the *Trieste,* a deep-sea research vessel owned by the U.S. Navy, descended to a depth of 35,802 feet (10,912 meters) in the Mariana Trench, setting a record.

Mid-Atlantic Ridge, Atlantic Ocean

The Mid-Atlantic Ridge is a divergent boundary that divides the floor of the Atlantic Ocean. It separates the North American Plate from the Eurasian Plate in its northern section and the South American Plate and the African Plate in its southern section. The submarine mountain range, which extends for about 10,000 miles (16,100 kilometers), is the longest mountain range on Earth. It lies about 10,000 feet (3,048 meters) below water level, except in a few areas where it surfaces as islands.

A slow-spreading mid-ocean ridge, it has a broad and deep central rift valley. The ridge, which ranges in width from 300 to 600 miles (483 to 965 kilometers), features many earthquakes and much volcanic activity. In a 500-mile (805-kilometer) segment of the ridge, geologists recorded a minimum of 481 seamounts.

The Mid-Atlantic Ridge began to develop almost 200 million years ago when the tectonic plates holding the present-day Americas, Europe, and Africa started to move away from each other. The Atlantic Ocean basin formed as a result, and it continues to widen.

For More Information

Books

Erickson, Jon. *Marine Geology: Exploring the New Frontiers of the Ocean.* Revised ed. New York: Facts on File, 2002.

Seibold, E., and W. H. Berger. *The Sea Floor.* Third ed. New York: Springer Verlag, 1996.

Web Sites

"Deep Ocean Basins." *COAST Resource Guide.* http://www.coast-nopp. org/visualization_modules/physical_chemical/basin_coastal_ morphology/principal_features/deep_ocean/basins.html (accessed on August 4, 2003).

"Harry Hammond Hess: Spreading the Seafloor." *U.S. Geological Survey.* http://pubs.usgs.gov/publications/text/HHH.html (accessed on August 4, 2003).

"Mid-Ocean Ridge." *Woods Hole Oceanographic Institute.* http://www.divediscover.whoi.edu/infomods/midocean/ (accessed on August 4, 2003).

"Ocean Regions: Ocean Floor-Characteristics." *Office of Naval Research.* http://www.onr.navy.mil/focus/ocean/regions/oceanfloor1.htm (accessed on August 4, 2003).

"The Sea Floor Spread." *Public Broadcasting Service.* http://www.pbs.org/wgbh/aso/tryit/tectonics/divergent.html (accessed on August 4, 2003).

"This Dynamic Earth: The Story of Plate Tectonics." *U.S. Geological Survey.* http://pubs.usgs.gov/publications/text/dynamic.html (accessed on August 4, 2003).

"World Ocean Floors." *Platetectonics.com.* http://www.platetectonics.com/oceanfloors/index.asp (accessed on August 4, 2003).

Plain

The topography or surface area of the world's continents varies greatly, with features ranging from mountains and other highland areas to plunging canyons and low-lying basins. Despite this diversity of landforms, certain large-scale features are common to all continents. Generally, the continents contain vast interior plains that make up over 50 percent of their landscape. Plains are also found along certain coasts of continents and on the ocean floor.

Plains may seem common and unremarkable, lacking the grand character of mountains or the mysteriousness of caves. Yet these normally flat landforms have a rich geological history, offering an insight into the forces that have helped shape the surface of the planet.

The shape of the land

A plain may be defined broadly as any lowland area that is level or gently sloping or rolling. It normally has few, if any, prominent hills or valleys, but may have considerable slope. A plain may be forested or bare of trees. Many plains around the world are covered in grasses. A plain may be as small as several hundred square feet or as large as hundreds of thousands of square miles.

A plateau is another landform that is relatively level, and some sources claim that a plateau is an elevated plain. A plateau has at least one steep, clifflike side. It forms as a result of geologic uplift (the slow upward movement of large parts of stable areas of Earth's crust due to heat forces within the planet) or as a result of many lava flows that spread out over hundreds of thousands of square miles. These flows, which build up the land surface, form plateaus known as lava or basalt plateaus because basalt is the dark, dense volcanic rock that forms these particular lava flows. (For further information, see the **Plateau** chapter.)

A plain may be defined as any lowland area that is level or gently sloping or rolling. Many plains around the world are covered in grasses. PHOTOGRAPH REPRODUCED BY PERMISSION OF THE CORBIS CORPORATION.

There are significant differences between a plateau and a plain. A plain has no steep sides, but sits at a low elevation relative to its surrounding landscape. It experiences no uplift. In fact, the heat forces within Earth, the actions of which have led to the formation of mountains, volcanoes, and plateaus, have played no direct role in the formation of plains. Those forces have broken Earth's crust (the thin, solid, outermost layer of the planet) and uppermost mantle (the region of the planet just below the crust) into sections or plates. The movement of the plates across the surface of the planet in response to the pressure exerted by those heat forces is known as tectonic activity (pronounced tek-TAH-nik; from the Greek word *tekton*, meaning "builder"). In contrast, plains are areas that are not tectonically active, but are quite stable.

Plains are formed primarily by erosion and the deposition of sediment. Erosion is the gradual wearing away of Earth surfaces through the action of wind and water. Sediment is rock debris such as clay, silt, sand, and gravel (or even larger material) that is being carried from its place of origin or has already been deposited on Earth's surface by wind, water, or ice.

Plains found on the interior of continents are known generally as interior or continental plains; those found along coasts are coastal plains.

Words to Know

Abyssal plain: The relatively flat area of an ocean basin between a continental margin and a mid-ocean ridge.

Alluvial fan: A fanlike deposit of sediment that forms where an intermittent, yet rapidly flowing canyon or mountain stream spills out onto a plain or relatively flat valley.

Alluvium: The general term for sediment (rock debris such as gravel, sand, silt, and clay) deposited by running water.

Coastal plain: A low, generally broad plain that lies between an oceanic shore and a higher landform such as a plateau or a mountain range.

Erosion: The gradual wearing away of Earth surfaces through the action of wind and water.

Fall line: The imaginary line that marks the sharp upward slope of land along a coastal plain's inland edge where waterfalls and rapids occur as rivers cross the zone from harder to softer rocks.

Floodplain: An area of nearly flat land bordering a stream or river that is naturally subject to periodic flooding.

Glacier: A large body of ice that formed on land from the compaction and recrystallization of snow, survives year to year, and shows some sign of movement downhill due to gravity.

Peneplain: A broad, low, almost featureless surface allegedly created by long-continued erosion.

Sedimentary rock: Rock that is formed by the accumulation and compression of sediment, which may consist of rock fragments, remains of microscopic organisms, and minerals.

Interior plains are frequently bounded on one or more sides by mountain ranges. Coastal plains, which cover less than 1 percent of the planet's total land area, generally rise from sea level until they meet higher landforms such as plateaus or mountain ranges. Some form narrow strips along coasts; others extend hundreds of miles inland. The imaginary line that marks the sharp upward slope of land along a coastal plain's inland edge where waterfalls and rapids occur as rivers cross the zone from harder to softer rocks is called the fall line. Some geologists now consider that term to be obsolete because materials that compose coastal plains are often found inland beyond that point.

Smaller-scale, level features formed by erosion and deposition are also labeled as plains. Glaciers, large bodies of ice that formed on land from the compaction and recrystallization of snow and survive year to year, deposit large amounts of sediment at their leading edges. This sediment forms broad, sweeping plains called outwash plains. (For further information on glaciers and their actions, see the **Glacial landforms and features** chapter.) Streams and rivers that periodically overflow the banks of their channels deposit sediment they are carrying on the surrounding landscape, creating floodplains. The general term for sediment deposited by running water is alluvium (pronounced ah-LOO-vee-em). Because floodplains are covered with alluvium, they are often called alluvial plains. Some sources use the term alluvial plain to describe any plain built up by sediments deposited by streams or sheets of running water. (For further information, see the **Floodplain** chapter.)

Abyssal (pronounced ah-BISS-ul) plains are relatively flat areas of ocean basins, which are that part of Earth's surface that extends seaward from the continental margins, the submerged outer edges of the continents. With gentle slopes of less than 1 foot (0.3 meter) of elevation difference for each 1,000 feet (305 meters) of distance, abyssal plains are far flatter than any plains on dry land. (For further information, see the **Ocean basin** chapter.)

A peneplain (pronounced PEE-nah-plane) is a broad, low, almost featureless surface allegedly created by long-continued erosion, which may include the action of glaciers or streams. Some sources state that peneplains descended from landforms that were originally rugged or much higher, such as plateaus or ancient mountains. These relatively flat surfaces are end products of the land surface after, supposedly, millions of years of erosion. This concept is troubling to many geologists, and the idea behind the formation of peneplains remains hotly debated.

Some sources incorrectly state that tundras, steppes, prairies, pampas, savannas, and llanos (pronounced YAH-nos) are plains. A plain is a landform; all of the others are biomes, which are distinct, natural communities chiefly distinguished by their plant life and climate. The confusion may be due to the fact that these biomes commonly cover plains.

Forces and changes: Construction and destruction

Fluvius is the Latin word meaning "river." Fluvial (pronounced FLEW-vee-ul) landforms are those shaped and created by running water. Because streams and other forms of running water are present in almost all landscapes, even if only occasionally, fluvial landforms dominate Earth's land surface. A highly effective means of erosion and transportation, running water carries billions of tons of sediment across the surface of the planet. Over a 1,000-year period, this is enough to lower land surfaces by an average of 1.3 inches (3.3 centimeters). It is a rate ample enough to level all continental land surfaces to a flat, featureless landscape in 25 million years.

The action of running water

Surging over a landscape, water picks up and transports as much material from the surface as it can carry. Gravity and steep slopes aid rushing water in carrying increasingly larger and heavier objects. Erosion by water begins as soon as raindrops hit the ground and loosen small particles. During heavy rains, sheets of water flow over the ground, loosening and picking up even more particles. This water quickly concentrates into channels, which then become streams that flow into rivers.

The amount and size of the material that running water can transport depends on the velocity or speed of that water. A fast-moving stream, for example, carries more sediment and larger material than a slow-moving one. A stream that is turbulent or agitated can also lift and carry more rocks and sediment than one that flows gently.

Running water will continue to carry its load of sediment as long as its velocity remains constant or increases (if it increases, it can carry an even larger load). Any change in the geography of the landscape that causes a water channel to bend or rise will slow the flow of the water. If running water loses speed, it loses the ability to carry its entire load and a portion will be deposited, depending on how much it slows down. Particles will be deposited by size with the largest settling out first and the finest deposited last.

The Literary Landscape

"On this continent and in the psyche of its peoples the plains have always been a staggering presence, a place of myth and cliche, a place for transformation, bafflement, or heartbreak. From the east they are release from the clawing of swamp and tangle and human density. From the west they are a drop and a straightening after the kinks and strains of mountains. Entered from any direction they are new air, a joy to behold, a combination of large-scale intimidation and primordial inner acoustics.

— **Merrill Gilfillan,** *Magpie Rising: Sketches from the Great Plains*, **1988.**

This is what occurs when streams and rivers overflow their banks to form floodplains. The water immediately loses velocity, and its load of sediment is deposited. As is always the case, larger particles drop out first, while finer-grained silts and clays are carried farther away from the stream or river channel.

Running water in high elevation areas, such as mountain ranges, flows rapidly down to lower-lying areas through canyons, valleys, and other narrow, confined channels. If the surface over which the water flows lacks plants and other ground cover, the rushing water easily picks up any loose material in its path.

When it finally reaches a lowland area, the running water loses power since gravity is no longer helping it flow down a steep slope. Slowing, the water is unable to carry the sediment it picked up on its way downhill. No longer confined to a narrow channel, the water spreads out the farther it moves away from the base of the mountain range. Large rocks and other heavy material are deposited first, followed by other material in decreasing size to form a fanlike deposit on the floor of the lowland. This deposit is known as an alluvial (pronounced ah-LOO-vee-al) fan.

Given time, as more water flows out, more sediment is deposited, and fans begin to merge with other fans. Over spans of millions of years, layer upon layer of sediment forms, spreading to cover thousands or hundreds of thousands of square miles, filling valleys, covering low hills, and leveling the land to form vast interior plains.

It is important to note that many interior plains, such as the Great Plains in the central United States, were once covered by ancient oceans and seas. As marine life perished, the remains settled to the bottom, where, over millions of years, they formed sedimentary rock (rock formed by the accumulation and compression of sediment, which may consist of rock fragments, remains of microscopic organisms, and minerals). When the waters receded, flat-lying layers of sedimentary rock remained, providing a somewhat level base for the further accumulation of sediment from nearby highland areas.

Coastal plains

Coastal plains are similarly covered by layers of sediment, these laid down by seaward-flowing streams from inland highland areas. Many coastal plains have a terraced landscape that stair-steps down to the coast. These gradually rising stairs are former shorelines and portions of sea bottom that emerged to become land. This landscape was formed over the last few million years as sea levels rose and fell in response to the repeated melting and growth of large continental glaciers. The weight of these immense glaciers also depressed land along coasts below sea level. When global temperatures rose and glaciers retreated, the land "rebounded," rising once again above sea level.

As continental glaciers lumbered across the landscape, they scoured away material underneath them, eroding and leveling the surface. They also plucked up rocks and other material, some of which were house-sized boulders. When the glaciers began to melt and retreat, they produced meltwater that flowed on top, within, and underneath the glaciers through channels. This meltwater moved large quantities of sediment from the glaciers. At the leading edges of the glaciers, the meltwater emerged in rapidly flowing, broad streams that surged away from the glaciers. The sediment in the meltwater was then deposited, forming outwash plains. Characteristically flat or gently rolling, outwash plains consist of layers of sand and other finely crushed sediments.

Spotlight on famous forms

Atlantic-Gulf Coastal Plain, United States

The Atlantic-Gulf Coastal Plain stretches over 3,200 miles (5,150 kilometers) in length from Cape Cod to Mexico. It is the world's largest

coastal plain, and it covers approximately 583,000 square miles (1,509,970 square kilometers). The coastal plain is divided into two regions in the United States. The Atlantic Coastal Plain stretches south from Cape Cod and the islands off southeast Massachusetts through New York, New Jersey, Delaware, Maryland, Virginia, North Carolina, South Carolina, Georgia, and Florida. Rounding Florida, it becomes the Gulf Coastal Plain, which continues through Alabama, Mississippi, Louisiana, Texas, and into Mexico.

The plain is narrow in New England but reaches a maximum width of about 200 miles (322 kilometers) farther south. While its terrain is mostly flat, it does slope gently seaward from the inland highlands in a series of terraces or ridges and low hills. This gentle slope continues far into the Atlantic Ocean and the Gulf of Mexico, forming the upper region of the continental margin, the submerged outer edge of the continent.

The Great Plains cover an area of about 450,000 square miles in central North America. **PHOTOGRAPH REPRODUCED BY PERMISSION OF THE CORBIS CORPORATION.**

Great Plains, United States

The Great Plains form an extensive grassland region in central North America. They stretch from the Canadian provinces of Alberta, Saskatchewan, and Manitoba south into Montana, North Dakota, South Dakota, Wyoming, Colorado, Nebraska, Kansas, Oklahoma, New Mexico, and northern Texas. They cover an area of about 450,000 square miles (1,165,500 square kilometers).

More than 65 million years ago, much of the present-day Great Plains was covered by a vast inland sea. Marine sediments that were deposited make up the nearly horizontal rock structure that underlies the area. When the Rocky Mountains began rising and the sea retreated, streams and rivers began to wash enormous amounts of sediment from the mountains over the plains. Currently, the plains slope gently eastward from that great mountain system at an elevation of 6,000 feet (1,829 meters). Where they merge into the interior lowlands, they stand at an elevation of approximately 1,500 feet (457 meters). The average eastward slope is roughly 10 feet per mile (1.9 meters per kilometer).

Glaciers from the last Ice Age left thick layers of sediment and other features that mark the landscape in the northern section of the Great Plains. In some places, the sediment measures to depths of hundreds of feet.

Although much of the terrain of the Great Plains is flat or gently rolling, several topographical features rise significantly above the plains. Prominent among these are the Black Hills of South Dakota and Wyoming, formed by an upwelling of magma under Earth's crust. They are one of the few indications of tectonic activity in this entire region.

West Siberian Plain, Russia

One of the world's largest regions of continuous flatland is found in central Russia. The West Siberian Plain lies between the Ural Mountains in the west and the Yenisey River Valley in the east. The Kara Sea bounds it in the north, while the Torghay Plateau, the Kazak Uplands, and the Altai Mountains mark its southern border. It stretches over a region nearly 1,100 miles (1,770 kilometers) wide, covering approximately 1.2 million square miles (3.1 million square kilometers).

Formed by glacial deposits after the last Ice Age, which ended approximately 10,000 years ago, the plain is exceedingly flat and featureless. Only occasional low hills and ridges, the remains of glacial action, punctuate the landscape. The plain has very poor drainage, resulting in vast swampy areas. The Vasyugan Swamp, in the center of the plain, covers 18,500 square miles (47,915 square kilometers). The northern section of the plain is mostly barren tundra.

For More Information

Web Sites

"Atlantic Plain Province." *U.S. Geological Survey and the National Park Service.* http://wrgis.wr.usgs.gov/docs/parks/province/atlantpl.html (accessed on August 6, 2003).

"The Great Plains and Prairies." *U.S. Department of State.* http://usinfo.state.gov/products/pubs/geography/geog11.htm (accessed on August 6, 2003).

"Interior Plains Province." *U.S. Geological Survey and the National Park Service.* http://wrgis.wr.usgs.gov/docs/parks/province/intplain.html (accessed on August 6, 2003).

Trimble, Donald E. "The Geologic Story of the Great Plains." *North Dakota State University Libraries.* http://www.lib.ndsu.nodak.edu/govdocs/text/greatplains/text.html (accessed on August 6, 2003).

The West Siberian Plain, which covers an area of about 1.2 million square miles, was formed by glacial deposits after the last Ice Age. **PHOTOGRAPH REPRODUCED BY PERMISSION OF THE CORBIS CORPORATION.**

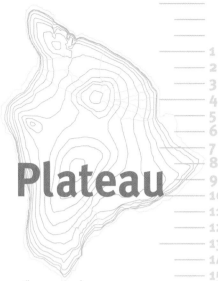

Plateau

1
2
3
4
5
6
7
8
9
10
11
12
13
14
15
16
17
18
19
20
21
22

Plateaus, known variously as tablelands or flat-topped mountains, are regions elevated thousands of feet above their surroundings. They are found on continents around the world, in countries ranging from Algeria to Mexico, from Mongolia to Zimbabwe. In Antarctica, which has a greater average elevation than any other continent, most of the land outside of the mountain ranges can be considered plateaus. Covered by thick ice, many of these areas have no names.

Some plateaus around the world exist at such great heights that their climate is harsh and living conditions are bleak. Others, at much lower elevations, offer more favorable conditions. The terrain of some plateaus is unbroken and flat. The terrain of many others has been eroded away by water and wind over millions of years to create distinct and unusual landforms. As such, many plateaus are landforms filled with landforms.

The shape of the land

By definition, a plateau is a relatively level, large expanse of land that rises some 1,500 feet (457 meters) or more above its surroundings and has at least one steep side. A plateau may cover an area as small as several square miles or as large as half the size of the lower forty-eight United States. Some plateaus formed as a result of geologic uplift, or the slow upward movement of large parts of stable areas of Earth's crust. Others lie between mountains, formed in response to the collision of sections of Earth's crust. Still others formed as a result of many lava flows that spread out over hundreds of thousands of square miles, building up the land surface. These latter plateaus are known as lava or basalt plateaus (basalt is the dark, dense volcanic rock that forms these particular lava flows). Some plateaus can form simply when the side of a land region is weathered away

The Colorado Plateau, which spans some 130,000 square miles, is actually made up of many plateaus.
PHOTOGRAPH REPRODUCED BY PERMISSION OF THE CORBIS CORPORATION.

through erosion (the gradual wearing away of Earth surface features through the action of wind and water).

Plateaus are widespread, covering about 45 percent of Earth's land surface. In Australia, approximately two-thirds of the land area is covered by the Western Plateau. This plateau continues unbroken across much of the central portion of the country, with only occasional rock outcroppings. Much of the plateau has existed as a landmass for more than 500 million years. About 25 percent of China's total land area may be characterized as plateau. The Tibetan Plateau in China's southwest region is the highest and most extensive plateau in the world.

As with all elevated areas, plateaus are continuously carved by erosion, the gradual wearing away of Earth's surfaces through the action of wind and water. Plateaus that contain rivers also contain canyons that have been cut by the rivers as they have sought to reach the level of the lake or ocean into which they flow. Finding the path of least resistance, a river winds across a plateau's surface, cutting through the rock layers. Over millions of years, a river will erode through and expose the rock layers of a plateau, creating a canyon. (For further information, see the **Canyon** chapter.)

Words to Know

Basalt: A dark, dense volcanic rock, about 50 percent of which is silica.

Continental drift: The hypothesis proposed by Alfred Wegener that the continents are not stationary, but have moved across the surface of Earth over time.

Convection current: The circular movement of a gas or liquid between hot and cold areas.

Crust: The thin, solid, outermost layer of Earth.

Erosion: The gradual wearing away of Earth surfaces through the action of wind and water.

Fault: A crack or fracture in Earth's crust along which rock on one side has moved relative to rock on the other.

Lithosphere: The rigid uppermost section of the mantle combined with the crust.

Mantle: The thick, dense layer of rock that lies beneath Earth's crust.

Plates: Large sections of Earth's lithosphere that are separated by deep fault zones.

Plate tectonics: The geologic theory that Earth's crust is composed of rigid plates that "float" toward or away from each other, either directly or indirectly, shifting continents, forming mountains and new ocean crust, and stimulating volcanic eruptions.

Uplift: In geology, the slow upward movement of large parts of stable areas of Earth's crust.

Plateaus may contain thousands of other landforms. Water is the primary sculpting force for most of these. In various forms (rain, groundwater, runoff, and rivers), water has carved mesas, buttes, domes, towers, hoodoos, goblins, temples, and natural rock arches and bridges across plateau landscapes (these landforms also appear elsewhere across the surface of Earth). In general, the relative hardness of the rock making up a plateau determines the type of landforms created there. If the plateau is built on sedimentary rock (rock formed by the accumulation and compression of sediment, which may consist of rock fragments, remains of microscopic organisms, and minerals), its layers will tend to be horizontal, and the landforms on it will have level or flat tops. If the plateau is built on different types of rock of varying hardness, its landforms may be flat or pointed.

Although a plateau is usually considered a single landmass, some plateaus may be composed of numerous smaller plateaus. Such is the case with the Colorado Plateau in the four-corners region (where the boundaries of the four states of Utah, Colorado, Arizona, and New Mexico meet) of the American Southwest. This plateau is actually a series of plateaus separated by north-south trending faults. A fault is a crack or fracture in Earth's crust along which rock on one side has moved relative to rock on the other. Unequal pressure beneath the Colorado Plateau, due to the heat forces contained within Earth, created stress in its surface. This resulted in faults. Separated by the faults, sections of the plateau moved upward by different degrees, creating differences in elevation across the plateau.

Forces and changes: Construction and destruction

The same internal forces of Earth responsible for mountain building, volcanic eruptions, earthquakes, seafloor spreading, and many other topographic features (physical features on the planet's surface) are also responsible for the creation of plateaus. To a lesser degree, so are external forces such as erosion, which helps define the steep sides of a plateau.

Earth is dynamic. As the planet revolves around the Sun and rotates on its axis, its surface and interior are also in motion. Landmasses are in a constant, though slow, state of change. They move, collide, and break apart due to the heat energy stirring beneath the surface of the planet. The giant furnace at Earth's core moves land no more than a few inches per year, but that is enough to have profound consequences on the shape of the landscape.

In the early twentieth century, German geophysicist Alfred Wegener (1880–1930) contended that Earth's continents do not remain in a fixed position on the planet's surface. He believed instead that they are mobile and over vast amounts of time have drifted across the surface. Wegener called his hypothesis continental drift. (A hypothesis is an educated guess, while a theory is a principle supported by extensive scientific evidence and testing.)

Wegener based his hypothesis on the idea that the coastlines of several of the world's continents fit remarkably together. From this, he proposed that the continents had once been joined together in one large continental mass. He called this supercontinent Pangaea (pronounced pan-JEE-ah; from the Greek words meaning "all lands"; see the box on page 255). What Wegener lacked, however, was a convincing explanation as to what moved the continents along the surface. Evidence to support his hypothesis did not come until the early 1960s when geologists developed the theory of plate tectonics.

Earth's layered interior

Geologists divide the surface and the interior of the planet into layers (see the illustration in Volume 1, page 63 of this set). The crust is the thin shell of rock that covers Earth. It is separated into two types: continental crust (which underlies the continents) and oceanic crust (which underlies the oceans). Varying in thickness from 3 to 31 miles (5 to 50 kilometers), the crust is thickest below land and thinnest below the oceans. Underneath the crust lies the mantle, which extends down roughly 1,800 miles (2,900 kilometers) beneath the planet's surface.

Pangaea: The Ancient Supercontinent

Throughout Earth's history, fragments of continental crust have floated across the planet's surface, pushed and pulled by plate tectonic motion. At times in the geologic past, these fragments (what we may now call continents) came together to form one large supercontinent, only to be broken apart once again by tectonic forces. The cycle of supercontinent construction and destruction took hundreds of millions of years.

The most recently created supercontinent was Pangaea (pronounced pan-JEE-ah), which came into being about 300 million years ago. Panthalassa, a giant ocean, surrounded it. In just 100 million years, though, Pangaea began to break apart. Tectonic forces created a north-south rift in the supercontinent, separating it into two new continents, Laurasia and Gondwanaland. As the new continents separated, the rift filled in with water, eventually becoming the present-day Atlantic Ocean.

Laurasia, composed of the present-day continents of Asia, Europe, and North America (Greenland), occupied the northern hemisphere. Gondwanaland, composed of the present-day continents of Africa, Antarctica, Australia, and South America, occupied the southern hemisphere. The subcontinent of India was also part of Gondwanaland. By 135 million years ago, the breakup of Laurasia and Gondwanaland was underway, leading to the present-day locations of the continents.

The forces that formed Pangaea, then broke it apart, are still at work. North America, South America, and Greenland are all moving westward. Australia, India, and the western part of Africa are all moving northward. Europe and Asia are moving eastward. The Atlantic Ocean is becoming larger, and the Pacific Ocean is becoming smaller. Although impossible to know when, at some point in the future, millions of years from now, the continents may well come together to form yet another supercontinent.

The mantle itself is separated into two distinct layers. The uppermost layer is cold and rigid. Geologists combine this section of the mantle with the overlying crust, calling it the lithosphere (pronounced LITH-uh-sfeer). The lithosphere measures roughly 60 miles (100 kilometers) thick. The part of the mantle immediately beneath the lithosphere is called the asthenosphere (pronounced as-THEN-uh-sfeer). This layer is composed of partially melted rock that has the consistency of putty and extends to a depth of about 155 miles (250 kilometers).

Beginning some 1,800 miles (2,900 kilometers) beneath the surface and extending to a depth of 3,960 miles (6,370 kilometers), the very center of the planet, is Earth's core. Composed of the metal elements iron and

Cultural Landforms

Above the floor of a deep sandstone canyon on the Rainbow Plateau in Utah, surrounded by cliffs that rise 1,000 feet (305 meters), spans the Rainbow Bridge. This natural sandstone bridge, 32 feet (10 meters) thick at its narrowest, arches 290 feet (88 meters) above the streambed of the Bridge Creek. Covering a distance of 270 feet (82 meters), Rainbow Bridge is the largest and most symmetrical natural bridge in the world.

Salmon-pink in color, the bridge is composed entirely of Navajo sandstone. Sandstone is a type of rock made up of grains of sand bonded together by a mineral cement, like calcium carbonate. Water easily dissolves this bond, washing away portions of the sand to form fascinating shapes. Million of years ago, water flowing off nearby Navajo Mountain washed over the area, cutting a canyon in the soft sandstone. As water continued to course through the canyon, it cut a hole in a curve in the canyon's side, eventually leading to the formation of the Rainbow Bridge.

For centuries, the Dine, Hopi, Paiute, and other Native American tribes have held the bridge and the area around it sacred. Present-day Navajo consider it a symbol of rainfall and fertility. In 1910, U.S. President William Howard Taft (1857–1930) designated the bridge and its immediate area a national monument. Currently, Rainbow Bridge is threatened by rising water from nearby Lake Powell Reservoir and by tourism.

nickel, the core has a solid inner portion and a liquid outer portion. Scientists estimate that temperatures in the core exceed 9,900°F (5,482°C), creating extreme heat energy. Were this energy not released in some manner, Earth's interior would melt. Circulating currents, called convection currents, carry the energy to the surface of the planet, where it is released. It is the release of this energy underneath the lithosphere that leads to the formation of the major geologic features on the surface of the planet.

Convection currents

Convection is the driving force behind the motion of Earth's interior. The process is similar to what occurs in a pot of boiling water. When the water reaches boiling temperature, normally 212°F (100°C) at sea level, it turns over and over. Heated water at the bottom of the pot rises to the surface because heating has caused it to expand and become less dense (lighter). Once at the surface, the heated material cools and becomes more dense (heavier), then sinks back down to the bottom to be reheated. This continuous motion of heated material rising, cooling, and sinking creates circular currents known as convection currents.

Rainbow Bridge National Monument, Utah. **PHOTOGRAPH REPRODUCED BY PERMISSION OF THE CORBIS CORPORATION.**

Convection currents form in the planet's interior when rock surrounding the core heats up. Expanding and becoming less dense, the heated rock slowly rises through cooler, denser rock that surrounds it in the mantle. When it reaches the lithosphere, the heated rock moves sideways along the bottom of the lithosphere, losing heat. As the rock cools and becomes denser, it sinks back toward the core, only to be heated once again. Scientists estimate that it takes about 200 million years for heated rock to make a circular trip from the core to the lithosphere and back again.

The slowly moving convection currents are able to release their heat energy near the surface of the planet because the lithosphere is not solid. It is broken into many large slabs or plates that "float" on the soft asthenosphere. In constant contact with each other, these plates fit together like a jigsaw puzzle. When one plate moves, other plates move in response. The pressure exerted by the convection currents underneath the lithosphere causes the plates to move toward or away from each other. Plate tectonics is the scientific theory explaining the plates and their movements and interactions.

Hoodoos on the Plateau

Hoodoo is a word used to refer to various forms of African-based folk magic and spiritual healing. It is also used to describe the strange and mystical rock shapes found in the western United States and Canada. The most remarkable hoodoos are found in Bryce Canyon in Utah, where erosion has shaped an enormous array of oddly shaped columns of rock tinted with countless subtle colors.

Water, ice, and gravity are the forces that formed Bryce Canyon and its unusual landforms. Yearly, the plateau area of the canyon receives about 19 inches (48 centimeters) of rain, which often falls in fierce thunderstorms. Unable to be absorbed by the normally dry soil, the water washes off in sheets and flash floods, eroding much of the soil and rock in its path. Water in the form of ice, however, is the greater erosive force in the canyon.

In addition to rain, approximately 100 inches (254 centimeters) of snow falls on the canyon per year. Water from the snow runs into cracks and joints in the canyon's rocks, then freezes at night. As water freezes into ice, it expands. The expanding ice in the cracks eventually breaks off portions of the rock, leaving behind a changed rock shape. This process is known as frost wedging.

The composition of the rocks of the hoodoos plays a further part in their bizarre-looking form. The hoodoos are composed of four different types of rock, each of which varies in hardness and erodes at a different rate. As different parts of the hoodoos erode at different times, the rock columns take on their wavy and pockmarked shape.

Plate tectonics and plateau formation

The plates making up the lithosphere have many different shapes and sizes. There are seven large plates, eight medium-sized plates, and a number of smaller plates. When the plates move, they interact with each other in one of three ways: they converge or move toward each other, they diverge or move away from each other, or they transform or slide past each other. Plate margins are the boundaries or areas where the plates meet and interact.

When two continental (land) plates converge, they crumple up and compress, forming complex mountain ranges and very high plateaus. This is the history of the Tibetan Plateau, created as a result of the collision between the Indian Plate and the Eurasian Plate. While the Himalayan Mountains formed along the edge of the collision, the plateau rose unbroken behind them.

When a continental plate and an oceanic plate converge, the oceanic plate (which is denser) slides beneath the continental plate in

Limestone hoodoos in Bryce Canyon National Park, Utah. **PHOTOGRAPH REPRODUCED BY PERMISSION OF THE CORBIS CORPORATION.**

a process known as subduction. As a plate subducts beneath another, its leading edge begins to melt because of high temperature and pressure in the mantle. This forms thick, flowing magma (molten rock beneath the planet's surface). Less dense than the rock that surrounds it deep underground, the magma rises toward Earth's surface, forcing its way through weakened layers of rock. In most instances, the magma collects in underground reservoirs called magma chambers. It remains there until enough pressure builds up to eject it onto the planet's surface through vents called volcanoes. (For further information, see the **Volcano** chapter.)

Sometimes the magma does not collect in a chamber, but rises beneath a large, stable landmass. Unable to break through any cracks or vents, the magma exerts pressure on the land, causing it to rise upward in one piece. Geologists believe this uplifting process formed the Colorado Plateau about five million years ago.

Lava plateaus

A lava plateau (also called a basalt plateau or flood basalt) is a special type of plateau, formed neither by the collision of continental plates nor by uplift. Instead, this layered plateau is built up over millions of years by lava repeatedly pouring forth through fissures, or long narrow cracks in the ground. (Lava is what magma is called once it reaches Earth's surface.) The cracks could be where tectonic plates are separating or where pressure from magma underneath the crust has created cracks in it.

The most abundant element found in magma is silicon, in the form of the oxide silica. (An oxide is a compound of an element and oxygen. As magma cools, the silica crystallizes to become the mineral quartz.) The amount of silica in magma determines how easily the magma flows. The higher the silica content, the slower the magma (lava) flows. Temperature also affects the flow rate of magma: the higher the magma's temperature, the more readily it flows.

The lava that floods the landscape to create a lava plateau is composed primarily of basalt, a hard, often glassy, black volcanic rock. Basalt has low silica content, and the lava it creates has a high temperature. These two properties combine to produce lava that flows quite rapidly. Erupting from cracks in the ground in thin sheets, basalt lava floods over the landscape, building up to form deposits thousands of feet thick.

The most famous example of a lava plateau in the United States is the Columbia Plateau. It covers most of southern Washington from its border with Idaho west to the Pacific Ocean and south into Oregon. The lava flows that accumulated to form the plateau occurred within the last seventeen million years. More than 40,700 square miles (170,000 square kilometers) of lava covers the plateau. In places, it measures 5,000 feet (1,524 meters) thick.

Spotlight on famous forms

Colorado Plateau, United States

Roughly circular, the Colorado Plateau sprawls across southeastern Utah, northern Arizona, northwestern New Mexico, and western Colorado. It covers a land area of 130,000 square miles (336,700 square kilometers). Only the states of Alaska, California, Montana, and Texas cover a larger area. While tectonic forces thrust the nearby Rocky Mountains into existence some forty to eighty million years ago, the Colorado Plateau remained structurally stable. Originally close to sea level, the plateau was slowly uplifted as a single mass approximately five million years ago.

Elevations on the plateau range from 3,000 to 14,000 feet (915 to 4,270 meters). The average elevation is 5,200 feet (1,585 meters).

Average yearly precipitation on the plateau is about 10 inches (25 cen-timeters). Because of the plateau's elevation and arid (dry) climate, there is limited plant cover. Erosion by wind and water has resulted in the cre-ation of many dramatic landforms. Rivers have cut thousands of miles of canyons within the plateau. Among these many canyons is the Grand Canyon, sculpted by the Colorado River. The pinnacles and spires of red rock in southwestern Utah's Bryce Canyon are among the most remark-able sights in the country.

An area of the state of Tamil Nadu in the west-ern portion of the Dec-can Plateau. The Deccan Plateau, which is largely made up of basalt lava, covers some 300,000 square miles in west-central India. **PHOTOGRAPH REPRODUCED BY PERMISSION OF PHOTO RESEARCHERS, INC.**

Deccan Plateau, India

The Deccan Plateau of west-central India is the oldest and most stable area of land in India. It is a lava plateau that formed over a period of one million or more years. Deccan comes from the Sanskrit work *dakshina*, meaning "south." The name is applied loosely to all elevated lands of southern India.

The relatively flat plateau covers some 300,000 square miles (770,000 square kilometers), encompassing the states of Andhra Pradesh, Karnataka, Kerala, and Tamil Nadu. Two mountain ranges, the Western and Eastern Ghats, flank it. In spots, the basalt lava flows that created it accumulated to a thickness of 6,000 feet (1,829 meters). In its western regions, the plateau averages about 2,500 feet (762 meters) in elevation; in its eastern parts, it averages 1,000 feet (305 meters). As a result of this difference in elevation from one side to the other, almost all rivers on the plateau flow from west to east and drain into the Bay of Bengal.

Siberian Traps, Russia

The largest volcanic eruptions in Earth's history occurred about 250 million years ago in present-day central Russia. In these eruptions, which scientists believe lasted for 200,000 to 1 million years, basalt lava flowed out of cracks in the ground, forming what is now known as the Siberian Traps. An enormous stretch of rolling land, it covers about 750,000 square miles (1,942,500 square kilometers). Heights on this vast plateau range from 1,600 to 2,300 feet (500 to 700 meters). The lava that created the Siberian Traps would form a layer 10 feet (3 meters) thick if spread out evenly across the planet.

Scientists speculate that the lava on the plateau came from magma that originated some 1,860 miles (3,000 kilometers) beneath Earth's crust. Some scientists have even argued that the rapid volcanic event behind the plateau's formation also brought about the largest extinction of animals in Earth's history. As many as 95 percent of all animal species on the planet were wiped out in an extinction that occurred around the same time period. The scientists point out that the dust and ash released by the lava flows could have blocked out the Sun's light, killing off plant life around the world, a necessary food source for animals. Or great amounts of carbon dioxide released by the flows could have encircled the planet, trapping the Sun's heat and raising temperatures worldwide, killing many life forms.

Tibetan Plateau, Tibet

The Tibetan Plateau is the highest and most widespread plateau in the world. Many believe it is probably the largest and highest area ever to exist in Earth's history. The plateau covers some 888,000 square miles (2.3

million square kilometers), an area roughly half that of the contiguous United States (connected forty-eight states). It is bounded on the north by the deserts of the Tarim and Qaidam (pronounced CHIE-dahm)Basins and on the south by the Himalayan Mountains.

Referred to as the "roof of the world," the plateau has an average elevation over 16,400 feet (5,000 meters). It contains fourteen mountains that rise higher than 26,248 feet (8,000 meters) and hundreds that rise more than 22,967 feet (7,000 meters). The Yarlung Zangbo River, which runs across the plateau, has cut the Yarlung Zangbo Grand Canyon, the deepest canyon in the world. The plateau itself is still geologically active and continues to rise, gaining an average of 0.04 inch (0.1 centimeter) per year in elevation.

Approximately forty to fifty million years ago, the northward-moving Indian Plate rammed into the Eurasian Plate, creating what would eventually become the Himalayan Mountains and the Tibetan Plateau. Geologists have long known that the crust beneath the plateau measures approximately 40 miles (65 kilometers) in depth, roughly twice that of the average continental crust. Only recently have scientists discovered that the plateau is supported by a bed of hot magma (molten rock). Since

The Tibetan Plateau is the highest and most widespread plateau in the world, with an average altitude of 16,400 feet. It also contains the two highest peaks in the world, Mount Everest and Mount K2, and has the deepest canyon in the world, the Yarlung Zangbo. **PHOTOGRAPH REPRODUCED BY PERMISSION OF THE CORBIS CORPORATION.**

magma is less dense (lighter) than cold, crustal rock, this bed of magma has helped raise the plateau as a single mass to such a great height.

For More Information

Books

Baars, Donald L. *A Traveler's Guide to the Geology of the Colorado Plateau.* Salt Lake City: University of Utah Press, 2002.

Ladd, Gary. *Landforms, Heart of the Colorado Plateau: The Story Behind the Scenery.* Las Vegas, NV: KC Publications, 2001.

Williams, David B. *A Naturalist's Guide to Canyon Country.* Helena, MT: Falcon Publishing Company, 2001.

Web Sites

"The Colorado Plateau: High, Wide, & Windswept." *BLM Environmental Education.* http://www.blm.gov/education/colplateau/index.html (accessed on September 2, 2003).

Geology of Tibet Plateau, the Roof of the World. http://www.100gogo.com/geo.htm (accessed on September 2, 2003).

"Lava Plateaus and Flood Basalts." *USGS.* http://vulcan.wr.usgs.gov/Glossary/LavaPlateaus/description_lava_plateaus.html (accessed on September 2, 2003).

Park Geology Tour: Colorado Plateau. http://www2.nature.nps.gov/grd/tour/cplateau.htm (accessed on September 2, 2003).

Stream and river

Flowing water, in streams and rivers or across the land in sheets, is the dominant erosional process in shaping Earth's landscape. Streams and rivers are not merely systems for moving surface water to the world's oceans and seas. They are also systems for moving weathered rocks and other sediment to those large bodies of water. In fact, it is estimated that streams and rivers move about 1.65 billion tons (1.5 billion metric tons) of sediment from land to the oceans each year. By shifting such great masses of sediment, streams and rivers become sculptors of the land.

Streams and rivers erode, transport sediment, change course, and flood their banks in natural and recurring patterns. It is true that most of the erosional work done by surface water is not done by streams or rivers but instead by falling raindrops and by the resulting unorganized runoff down slopes. Yet streams and rivers are able to create both erosional landforms (their own channels, canyons, and valleys) and depositional landforms (floodplains, alluvial fans, and deltas) as they flow over Earth's surface.

The shape of the land

Geologists define a stream as any body of running water that moves downslope under the influence of gravity in a narrow and defined channel on Earth's surface. Streams are also found on the ground surface in caves and underneath and inside glaciers (large bodies of ice that formed on land by the compaction and recrystallization of snow and that survive year to year). Rivers, creeks, brooks, and runs are all streams. Most sources define a river simply as a large stream; creeks, brooks, and runs are simply small streams. For this discussion, stream will be used to refer to all of these bodies of running water.

The waters of almost half a continent flow through the Mississippi River. About 159 million tons of sediment—70 percent of which consists of clay, silt, and fine sand—are carried by the river annually. PHOTOGRAPH REPRODUCED BY PERMISSION OF THE CORBIS CORPORATION.

When water flows down a slope, it tends to gather in small depressions on the surface along the way. This concentration of moving water stimulates the process of erosion, which is the gradual wearing away of Earth surfaces through the action of wind and water. As the water erodes rock and other material in the depression, it forms a channel. The stream channel is the landform, not the water carried in it. The sides of the channel are known as the stream's banks. The bottom is the stream bed.

A stream's velocity, or speed, determines its ability to erode, transport, and deposit sediment. Sediment is rock debris such as clay, silt, sand, gravel, or even larger material. Alluvium (pronounced ah-LOO-vee-em) is the general term for sediment deposited by running water. A fast-moving stream carries more sediment and larger material than a slow-moving one. A stream that is turbulent, with water whirling through the channel and not flowing in a steady and straight manner, can also lift and carry

Words to Know

Alluvial fan: A fanlike deposit of sediment that forms where an intermittent, yet rapidly flowing, canyon or mountain stream spills out onto a plain or relatively flat valley.

Alluvium: The general term for sediment (rock debris such as gravel, sand, silt, and clay) deposited by running water.

Base level: The level below which a stream cannot erode.

Bed load: The coarse sediment rolled along the bottom of a stream.

Channel: The depression where a stream flows or may flow.

Cut bank: A steep, bare slope formed on the outside of a meander.

Delta: A body of sediment deposited at the mouth of a stream where it enters an ocean or a lake.

Dissolved load: Dissolved substances, the result of the chemical weathering of rock, that are carried along in a stream.

Distributaries: The channels that branch off of the main stream in a delta, carrying water and sediment to the delta's edges.

Erosion: The gradual wearing away of Earth surfaces through the action of wind and water.

Floodplain: An area of nearly flat land bordering a stream that is naturally subject to periodic flooding.

Graded stream: A stream that is maintaining a balance between the processes of erosion and deposition.

Groundwater: Freshwater lying within the uppermost parts of Earth's crust, filling the pore spaces in soil and fractured rock.

Levee (natural): A low ridge or mound along a stream bank, formed by deposits left when floodwater slows down on leaving the channel.

Meander: A bend or loop in a stream's course.

Oxbow lake: A crescent-shaped body of water formed from a single loop that was cut off from a meandering stream.

Point bar: The low, crescent-shaped deposit of sediment on the inside of a meander.

Rapids: The section of a stream where water flows fast over hard rocks.

River: A large stream.

Stream: Any body of running water that moves downslope under the influence of gravity in a defined channel on Earth's surface.

Suspended load: The fine-grained sediment that is suspended in the flow of water in a stream.

Waterfall: A steep drop in a stream bed causing the water in a stream channel to fall vertically or nearly vertically.

more rocks and sediment than one that flows gently. Turbulence is due to the friction caused by rocks and steps in the stream's channel.

Factors that influence the velocity of a stream include its gradient (slope of its channel), the amount of sediment it carries, the shape of its channel, and its discharge (volume of water flowing past a given point over a given period of time). A low gradient, a high amount of sediment, a rough channel (both bed and banks), and a low discharge will all slow the velocity of a stream.

A stream's load is the total amount of sediment it is carrying. The sediment load consists mainly of two parts. The first part is the coarse material such as sand and gravel that moves along the stream bed. This is known as the bed load. As it is carried along, this coarse sediment acts as an abrasive, scouring and wearing away the banks and bed of the stream. The stream then picks up any newly loosened and eroded material. The second part is the fine-grained material such as clay and silt that is suspended in the water as the stream flows along. This is the suspended load. Streams also carry a dissolved load. These dissolved substances are the result of the chemical weathering of rock, which alters the internal structure of minerals by removing or adding elements.

Stream channels

There are three types of stream channels: straight, meandering, and braided. Although there are no absolutely straight channels in nature, geologists refer to straight channels as those that are relatively straight with little lateral or side-to-side movement. They are typically found in the headlands, or area where the stream begins, usually a highland or mountainous region. They are also found following an underlying weak rock layer in an area, such as along a fault or a joint (a fault is a crack or fracture in Earth's crust along which rock on one side has moved relative to rock on the other; when no movement has occurred, the fracture is known as a joint). The velocity of the water in a straight channel is fast because the channel often has a steep gradient. Its discharge is also high. The channel is often deeper than it is wide, and most erosion occurs along the stream bed, although its sediment load is not yet large.

Meandering stream channels are quite common. In fact, virtually all flowing fluids meander. Jet streams, the fast upper-air winds that travel west-to-east around the planet, meander. So does the Gulf Stream, the warm surface ocean current that originates in the Gulf of Mexico and flows northeast across the Atlantic Ocean. In a meandering channel, the erosional energy of the water is directed side to side instead of downward, and so the channel moves across the landscape like a wiggling snake. (See the photo on page 269.) The series of S-shaped bends are called meanders (pronounced me-AN-ders; the term comes from the Menderes River in southwest Turkey, noted for its winding course). The velocity of the water is highest and the water level deepest on the outer parts of the meanders. High velocities and greater turbulence result in erosion as the stream eats into its bank, creating eroded areas called cut banks. Along the inner parts of the meanders, where the water level is shallow and velocity is slow, sediment is deposited to form crescent-shaped point bars. If erosion on the outside of a meander continues to take place, eventually the meander can become cut off from the rest of the stream. When this occurs, the separated

meander forms a body of water called an oxbow lake. (For further information, see the **Floodplain** chapter.)

When a stream's discharge varies frequently and its sediment load is large, the sediment may be deposited to form bars and islands within the main channel. The water then flows around these deposits in small channels, which unite farther downstream. This type of channel is called a braided stream channel because the many crisscrossing smaller channels resemble hair braids. When discharge increases in the channel, the bars and islands may be covered or eroded and redeposited once the discharge decreases again. If vegetation takes hold on the bars or islands, these features may not be easily eroded.

Erosional features

The course of a stream's channel can be affected if the rock layer over which it passes changes from a hard, resistant layer to one that is weaker and more easily eroded. As the softer material is worn away, the resistant rock remains as a step or ledge over which the water in the channel flows. This drop in the stream bed that causes the water to fall vertically or nearly vertically is called a waterfall. Often the drop is steep. A waterfall may also develop where a stream flows over the edge of a plateau or in

The meandering Tigre River, Argentina.
PHOTOGRAPH REPRODUCED BY PERMISSION OF THE CORBIS CORPORATION.

Earth's Tallest Waterfalls

Waterfall	Height	Location
Angel Falls	3,212 feet (979 meters)	Venezuela
Tugela Falls	3,110 feet (948 meters)	South Africa
Tyssestrengene	2,795 feet (852 meters)	Norway
Browne Falls	2,744 feet (836 meters)	New Zealand
Utigardsfossen	2,625 feet (800 meters)	Norway
Colonial Creek Falls	2,584 feet (788 meters)	Washington, USA
Mtarazi Falls	2,499 feet (762 meters)	Zimbabwe
Yosemite Falls	2,425 feet (739 meters)	California, USA
Espelandsfossen	2,307 feet (703 meters)	Norway
Mongefossen	2,296 feet (700 meters)	Norway

areas where glaciers have eroded deep valleys in mountainous terrain and streams flowing from higher parts plunge to the valley floor. In a waterfall, as water continues to fall over the edge, it erodes the bed of the channel at the base of the waterfall. A basin or depression is created, and sediment carried by the stream is deposited here. Depending on their hardness, the rock layers behind the falling water may also be eroded over time by the action of the water. As these softer layers are cut into, the resistant layer under the bed of the stream ultimately loses support and falls into the water at the base of the waterfall. When this occurs, the waterfall retreats farther upstream.

Normally, over time, the stream will erode the resistant rock so the gradient of the channel is not as steep. The waterfall will be reduced to rapids, an area where water in the stream channel rushes downward over hard rocks. The reduction of a major waterfall to rapids may take tens of thousands of years. Eventually, the rapids, too, will be eroded away.

Other erosional features created by streams are canyons and V-shaped valleys. On plateaus and in mountains, a stream erodes a fairly narrow path through the landscape, often only as wide as its channel. It does so because most of its erosional force is directed along its bed. As the stream erodes downward, a process referred to as downcutting, steep slopes remain on either side of the stream's channel. If the stream is cutting through a region composed of rocks that are highly resistant to erosion, a narrow, steep-walled canyon is created. (For further information, see the **Canyon** chapter.) If the rocks in the region are more susceptible to erosion, rockslides and other types of landslides gradually modify the steep slopes to form a V-shaped valley. (For further information, see the **Valley** chapter.)

Depositional features

In addition to bars and islands in braided streams and point bars in meandering streams, streams create larger features by depositing sediment. Among these are floodplains, alluvial fans, and deltas.

When the flow of water in a stream becomes too high to be accommodated in the stream's channel, the water flows over the stream's banks and floods the surrounding land. As it does so, the water immediately slows down and drops its sediment load. Coarser sediment is deposited near the channel. Over time, as the process is repeated over and over, the sediment forms mounds called natural levees along the stream's banks. Finer sediment carried by the flood is spread farther away from the channel before it is finally deposited. The flat or gently sloping surface created by the repeated deposition of sediment along a stream is called the stream's floodplain. A floodplain is widened as a stream meanders across a landscape. (For further information, see the **Floodplain** chapter.)

When a stream whose channel has been confined in a narrow valley or canyon in a highland area flows out into a broader, flatter valley or plain, its velocity and gradient suddenly decrease. No longer confined to a narrow channel, the water spreads farther as it moves away from the base of the highlands. Large rocks and other heavy material are deposited first, followed by other material in decreasing size. As more water flows onto the valley and more sediment is deposited, a wide, fan-shaped pile known as an alluvial fan forms.

When a stream enters a body of standing water, such as an ocean or a lake, again there is a sudden decrease in velocity. The stream drops its sediment load in a deposit called a delta. Deltas build outward from a coastline, but will survive only if ocean currents are not strong enough to remove the sediment. As the velocity of a stream decreases on entering the delta, the stream becomes choked with sediment, similar to what occurs in a braided stream channel. Instead of braiding, however, the stream channel breaks into many smaller channels called distributaries that carry water and sediment to the delta's edges. (For further information, see the **Delta** chapter.)

Forces and changes: Construction and destruction

Water running down a slope becomes a stream when there is enough water to form a tiny rivulet with a channel to contain the water. In its early stage, a stream may carry water only after rain falls or snow melts. In this instance, it is said to be an intermittent stream. In contrast, a permanent stream is one that has cut its valley deeply enough so that groundwater seeps into it and keeps it flowing between rainfalls. Beneath Earth's surface, water fills the pore spaces and openings in rocks. This water,

The Literary Landscape

"The overall impression here, as one surveys the river spread out over the gravel bars, is of a suspension of light, as though light were reverberating on a membrane. And a loss of depth. The slope of the riverbed here is nearly level, so the movement of water slows; shallowness heightens the impression of transparency and a feeling for the texture of the highly polished stones just underwater. If you bring your eye to within a few inches of the surface, each stone appears to be submerged in glycerin yet still sharply etched, as if held closely under a strong magnifying glass in summer light."

—**Barry Holstun Lopez, *River Notes: The Dance of Herons*, 1979.**

which comes from rain or melted snow that is drawn downward through the soil by gravity, is known as groundwater. At a certain level below ground, all the openings in the rocks are completely filled with groundwater. The upper surface of this saturated zone is known as the water table.

A stream has a natural tendency to reach a base level. This refers to the point at which the stream reaches the elevation of the large body of water, such a lake or ocean, into which it drains. Aided by gravity, a stream flows toward the level of its final destination as quickly as possible. The larger the difference in height between the stream and its destination, the greater the erosive or cutting force of the stream. For most larger streams, base level is sea level. For tributaries, smaller streams that flow into larger ones, base level is the entry point where they empty into the larger stream.

Streams erode because they have the ability to pick up sediment and transport it to a new location. That sediment may come from several sources: It may have been eroded from the bed and banks of the stream, or it may have fallen into the stream after moving (slowly or quickly) down a slope bordering the stream's channel.

A stream erodes through two actions: hydraulic action and abrasion. Hydraulic action is the force exerted by the water itself. It tends to work along the banks of streams, attacking and undermining layers of soil and rock. Abrasion is the grinding and scraping of the stream's banks and bed by the sediment carried in the stream as the suspended load and bed load.

The amount of sediment a stream moves depends on the velocity of the stream and the size of the sediment particles. Water moving at a low velocity can move only small, fine particles such as sand, silt, and clay. Sand is a mineral particle with a diameter between 0.002 and 0.08 inch (0.005 and 0.2 centimeter); silt is a mineral particle with a diameter between 0.00008 and 0.002 inch (0.0002 and 0.005 centimeter); clay is a mineral particle with a diameter less than 0.00008 inch (0.0002 centimeter). Water moving at a high velocity can move both small particles and large, coarse particles such as boulders.

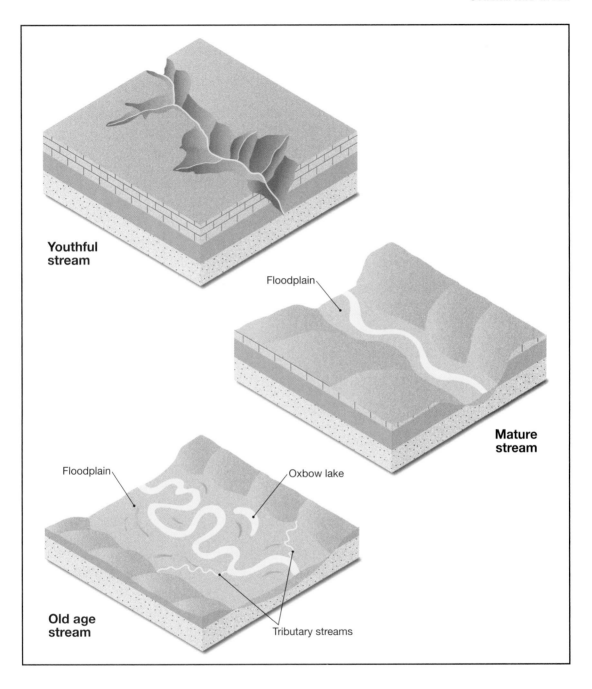

Youthful
stream

Floodplain

Mature
stream

Floodplain

Oxbow lake

Old age
stream

Tributary streams

A stream will continue to carry its load as long as its velocity remains constant or increases (if it increases, it can carry an even larger load). Any change in the geography of the landscape that causes a stream channel to bend or rise (lessening its gradient) will slow the flow of water in the

Stages of stream development: a youthful stream, mature stream, and old age stream.

channel. As soon as a stream's velocity decreases, it loses the ability to carry all of its load and a portion will be deposited, depending on how much the stream slows down. Particles will be deposited by size with the largest settling out first.

Stream stages

Geologists characterize streams as youthful, mature, and old. Typically, streams have steep gradients near their sources, or beginnings, and gentle gradients as they approach their mouths, or ends. Discharge increases downstream as more tributaries connect with main streams as they flow toward their base levels. Because of this, stream channels also become deeper and wider downstream.

A youthful stream has a fairly straight channel and a steep gradient. It generally flows in a V-shaped valley in a highland or mountainous area with little shifting of its channel. Its velocity is high, and it is actively lowering its channel through downcutting in order to reach base level. In this stage, a stream has little, if any, floodplain. Rapids and waterfalls may mark its course.

A stream in its mature stage has a moderate gradient and velocity because it has eroded its bed downward and is closer to base level. Since it has slowed down, the stream begins to meander. While it is still eroding downward, the stream's main force of erosion is lateral (horizontal) as it begins winding back and forth, carving out a valley floor between valley walls or bluffs. Periodically, the stream will flood all or a part of its valley, depositing alluvium on its developing floodplain.

An old age stream has nearly reached its base level, and its gradient and velocity are very low. Because its velocity is low, it has lost its ability to erode downward. In fact, it deposits as much material as it erodes. The stream meanders greatly in its nearly flat valley. It has a wide, well-developed floodplain marked with oxbow lakes.

Graded stream

A stream with the correct gradient and channel characteristics to maintain the velocity required to transport its sediment load is known as a graded stream. It is a stream that is in equilibrium or balance. On average, it is neither eroding nor depositing sediment but simply transporting it. This involves a balance among base level, discharge, channel shape or size, and sediment load. Any changes to one or more of these by some event—lowering of sea level, the uplift of a land area containing a stream, the blocking of a stream channel by natural or artificial means—will result in erosion or deposition until a new balanced state is reached.

Spotlight on famous forms

Amazon River, Peru and Brazil

The Amazon River is the world's second longest river (the Nile River in Africa is the longest). It runs for about 3,900 miles (6,275 kilometers) from the Andes Mountains in northern Peru to the Atlantic Ocean near Belem, Brazil. When it enters the ocean, the Amazon discharges about 7,000,000 cubic feet (198,450 cubic meters) of water per second. The width of the Amazon ranges from about 1 to 8 miles (1.6 to 13 kilometers).

Although the Amazon is usually only about 20 to 40 feet (6 to 12 meters) deep, there are narrow channels where it can reach a depth of 300 feet (91 meters). Almost every year, the Amazon floods, filling a floodplain up to 30 miles (48 kilometers) wide. The fresh layer of sediment deposited by the flood makes the surrounding region extremely fertile.

The Amazon basin (the area drained by the Amazon River) is the largest river basin in the world. It covers an area of about 2,500,000 square miles (6,475,000 square kilometers), or almost 35 percent of the land area of South America. The volume of water that flows from the basin into the Atlantic is about 11 percent of all the water drained from all the continents of Earth.

The world's second longest river, the Amazon, runs for about 3,900 miles through Peru and Brazil. **PHOTOGRAPH REPRODUCED BY PERMISSION OF THE CORBIS CORPORATION.**

The Iguazú Falls, located on the border between Argentina and Brazil, is composed of 275 waterfalls that are strung out along the rim of a crescent-shaped cliff about 2.5 miles long. PHOTOGRAPH REPRODUCED BY PERMISSION OF THE CORBIS CORPORATION.

Iguazú Falls, Argentina and Brazil

From its source in the mountains not far from the Atlantic Ocean, the Iguazú (pronounced ee-gwah-ZOO) River flows westward across southern Brazil before entering Argentina and Paraguay. In the language of the native people of the region, Iguazú means "great waters." Along its 745-mile (1,200-kilometer) course, the river flows over 70 waterfalls as it seeks its base level.

The most famous of these waterfalls is located on the border between Argentina and Brazil. The Iguazú Falls is composed of 275 individual falls strung out along the rim of a crescent-shaped cliff about 2.5 miles (4 kilometers) long. The river drops 269 feet (82 meters) at the falls. The water in the river flows over the edge of the falls at an average rate of 553 cubic feet (17 cubic meters) per second.

The falls were created nearly 100,000 years ago when a volcanic eruption produced a lava flow that stopped abruptly, forming a huge, natural cliff.

Volga River, Russia

The Volga River in western Russia is the longest river in Europe. It begins in the Valdai Hills northwest of Moscow and flows for about 2,200 miles (3,530 kilometers) before forming a great delta where it enters the

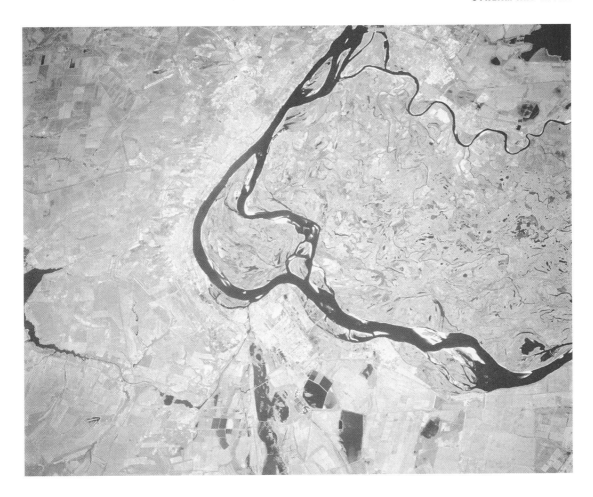

Caspian Sea. Its source is only 740 feet (226 meters) above sea level. Combined with its many tributaries, the Volga River drains an area of over 502,000 square miles (1,300,000 square kilometers).

Much of the water that flows in the Volga River comes from snowmelt. Many large dams have been built on the river to provide hydro-electricity and water for irrigation. Prior to the dams being built, the river carried an estimated 25.5 million tons (23 metric tons) of sediment to the Caspian Sea. The dams have also reduced the amount of natural floods along the river and the velocity of the river's flow.

The Volga River, in Russia, is the longest river in Europe, running for some 2,200 miles. **PHOTOGRAPH REPRODUCED BY PERMISSION OF THE CORBIS CORPORATION.**

For More Information

Books

Leopold, Luna B. *A View of the River.* Cambridge, MA: Harvard University Press, 1994.

Leopold, Luna B. *Water, Rivers and Creeks*. Sausalito, CA: University Science Books, 1997.

Martin, Patricia A. Fink. *Rivers and Streams*. New York: Franklin Watts, 1999.

Schuh, Mari C. *What Are Rivers?* Mankato, MN: Pebble Books, 2002.

Web Sites

"Earth's Water: River and Streams." *U.S. Geological Survey*. http://ga.water.usgs.gov/edu/earthrivers.html (accessed on August 14, 2003).

RiverResource. http://riverresource.com/ (accessed on August 14, 2003).

"Rivers and Streams." *Missouri Botanical Garden*. http://mbgnet.mobot. org/fresh/rivers/index.htm (accessed on August 14, 2003).

"River World." *Kent National Grid for Learning*. http://www.kented.org. uk/ngfl/rivers/index.html (accessed on August 14, 2003).

"Virtual River." *Geology Labs On-line Project*. http://vcourseware. sonoma.edu/VirtualRiver/ (accessed on August 14, 2003).

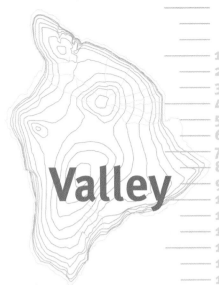

Valley

Valleys are one of the most common landforms on the surface of the planet. They are carved by flowing water or flowing ice through the process of erosion, which is the gradual wearing away of Earth surfaces through the action of wind and water. Valleys take on a wide variety of forms—from steep-sided canyons, such as the Grand Canyon on the Colorado River, to broad plains, such as the lower Mississippi River valley. The form of a valley depends on many factors, including what is eroding it, the slope of the land surface, the nature of the soil or rock where the valley is being created, and time.

The shape of the land

A valley is a relatively large hollow or depression bounded by hills or mountains on Earth's surface that is developed by stream erosion or glacial activity and that is drained externally. A basin is another hollow or depression on Earth's surface, but it has no outlet to drain the water. (For further information, see the **Basin** chapter.) Geologists refer to any body of running water moving downslope in a defined channel as a stream (a river is a large stream). A glacier is a large body of ice that formed on land by the compaction and recrystallization of snow, survives year to year, and shows some sign of movement downhill due to gravity. The three main types of valleys are the V-shaped valley, the flat-floored valley, and the U-shaped valley.

A V-shaped valley is a narrow valley that has a profile suggesting the form of the letter "V," characterized by steeply sloping sides. It results from a stream eroding downward, a process referred to as downcutting. V-shaped valleys form in mountains or other highland areas where streams are in their beginning or "youthful" stage and are flowing rapidly down steep slopes. The bottom of a valley is called its floor. In highland areas

Blue Ridge Mountain Valley, North Carolina. Valleys are carved by flowing water or flowing ice through the process of erosion, which is the gradual wearing away of Earth surfaces through the action of wind and water.
PHOTOGRAPH REPRODUCED BY PERMISSION OF THE CORBIS CORPORATION.

Words to Know

Alpine glacier: A relatively small glacier that forms in high elevations near the tops of mountains.

Base level: The level below which a stream cannot erode.

Erosion: The gradual wearing away of Earth surfaces through the action of wind and water.

Fjord: A deep glacial trough submerged with seawater.

Floodplain: An area of nearly flat land bordering a stream that is naturally subject to periodic flooding.

Glacial trough: A U-shaped valley carved out of a V-shaped stream valley by the movement of a valley glacier.

Glacier: A large body of ice that formed on land by the compaction and recrystallization of snow, survives year to year, and shows some sign of movement downhill due to gravity.

Hanging valley: A shallow glacial trough that leads into the side of a larger, main glacial trough.

Levee (natural): A low ridge or mound along a stream bank, formed by deposits left when floodwater slows down on leaving the channel.

Mass wasting: The spontaneous movement of material down a slope in response to gravity.

Meander: A bend or loop in a stream's course.

Rift valley: The deep central crevice in a mid-ocean ridge; also, a valley or trough formed between two normal faults.

Stream: Any body of running water that moves downslope under the influence of gravity in a defined channel on Earth's surface.

U-shaped valley: A valley created by glacial erosion that has a profile suggesting the form of the letter "U," characterized by steep sides that may curve inward at their base and a broad, nearly flat floor.

Valley glacier: An alpine glacier flowing downward through a preexisting stream valley.

V-shaped valley: A narrow valley created by the downcutting action of a stream that has a profile suggesting the form of the letter "V," characterized by steeply sloping sides.

near a stream's source, or beginning, the valley sides slope down almost directly to the stream's banks, or sides of its channel. The valley floor in this region is narrow or even nonexistent.

Downstream, as the gradient or slope of the stream's channel lessens and becomes more gentle, the floor of the valley widens. A stream in this stage is no longer considered youthful but "mature." A stream flowing at a moderate to low gradient tends to erode more along the banks of its channel than along its bed or bottom. Thus, the stream slowly sweeps across the valley floor in a series of S-shaped bends called meanders (pronounced me-AN-ders). Over time, as the stream continues to meander, it erodes away material on the valley floor, ever widening it. The shape of the valley changes progressively from a sharp V to a broader V to one that has a flat floor. This latter type of valley, with a floor that is horizontal and often wide, is known as a flat-floored valley. This type of valley is the most common.

Streams are systems for moving sediment—rock debris such as clay, silt, sand, gravel, or even larger material—across Earth's surface to the world's oceans and seas. Naturally and routinely, the flow of water in a stream may become too high to be accommodated in the stream's channel. The water then flows over the stream's banks and floods the surrounding land. As it does so, the water immediately slows down and drops any sediment it was carrying. Coarser sediment is deposited near the channel. Over time, as the process is repeated over and over, the sediment forms mounds called natural levees along the stream's banks. Finer sediment (sands, silt, and clay) carried by the water is spread farther away from the channel before it is finally deposited. The flat or gently sloping surface created by the repeated deposition of sediment along a stream is called the stream's floodplain. A floodplain may cover all or just a portion of the valley floor. (For further information, see the **Stream and river** and **Floodplain** chapters.)

A U-shaped valley is a valley that has a profile suggesting the form of the letter "U," characterized by steep sides that may curve inward at their bases and a broad, nearly flat floor. Specifically, a U-shaped valley is one carved by glacial erosion. Thick masses of ice that move slowly over Earth's surface, glaciers are found in regions close to the North and South Poles, the extreme northernmost and southernmost points on the globe, or in mountains at high elevations. Those that form over large areas of continents close to the poles are called continental glaciers or ice sheets. Two continental glaciers are found on Earth: one covers 85 percent of Greenland in the Northern Hemisphere and the other covers more than 95 percent of Antarctica in the Southern Hemisphere. Relatively small glaciers that form in high elevations near the tops of mountains are called alpine or mountain glaciers. (For further information, see the **Glacial landforms and features** chapter.)

Because of their size and weight, continental glaciers destroy topography, leveling the surface features of a landscape. The effect of alpine glaciers is not as extreme. They flow down pre-existing V-shaped valleys created by streams to form U-shaped valleys. Because of this, they are also known as valley glaciers. Whereas a stream only occupies the floor (or a main portion of it) in a V-shaped valley, a valley glacier occupies the entire valley, eroding both the sides and the floor as it moves, deepening and widening the valley. U-shaped valleys are also known as glacial troughs.

Draining an area, streams tend to flow across the landscape in a tree-like pattern: the smallest streams (the outer branches) flow into larger streams (the inner branches), which flow into the main stream (the trunk). Smaller streams that flow into larger ones are known as tributaries. When valley glaciers fill an area, they may occupy the valleys created

U-shaped valley in Zion National Park, Utah.
PHOTOGRAPH REPRODUCED BY PERMISSION OF FIELD MARK PUBLICATIONS.

by a main stream and its nearest tributaries. Tributary valleys almost always join the main stream valley at the same altitude or height, but glacial action deepens the main valley more than its side valleys. The shallower glacial troughs created by these smaller valley glaciers (known as tributary glaciers) are called hanging valleys. If temperatures in the area increase, causing the glaciers to melt and retreat, meltwater from the glaciers may form streams that run through these hanging valleys. In spectacular instances, streams in hanging valleys often fall to the floor of the main valley as a waterfall.

In certain instances, a valley glacier may flow all the way to a coastline, carving out a deep, narrow U-shaped valley. If the glacier melts, the valley may become flooded with seawater, forming an inlet known as a fjord (pronounced fee-ORD).

The term rift valley is used to describe an area where a section of Earth's crust (thin, solid outermost layer of the planet) has dropped down between two normal faults (cracks or fractures in Earth's crust along which rock on one side has moved relative to rock on the other). Essentially, whenever the planet's crust is subjected to compression or tension caused by heat forces beneath the crust, faults develop, and some blocks of rock

The Literary Landscape

"The famous Yosemite Valley lies at the heart of it, and it includes the head waters of the Tuolumne and Merced rivers, two of the most songful streams in the world; innumerable lakes and waterfalls and silky lawns; the noblest forests, the loftiest granite domes, the deepest ice-sculptured cañon, the brightest crystalline pavements, the snowy mountains soaring into the sky twelve and thirteen thousand feet, arrayed in open ranks and spiry pinnacled groups partially separated by tremendous cañons and amphitheatres; gardens on their sunny brows, avalanches thundering down their long, white slopes, cataracts roaring gray and foaming in the crooked rugged gorges, and glaciers in their shadowy recesses working in silence, slowly completing their sculpture; new-born lakes at their feet, blue and green, free or encumbered with drifting icebergs like miniature Arctic Oceans, shining, sparkling, calm as stars."

—John Muir, *Our National Parks*, 1901.

drop along these fractures relative to the ground on either side. A rift valley is not a true valley. The dropped-down block or crust that formed a depression on the surface of the ground is correctly called a graben (pronounced GRAH-bin). Rift valleys, which are found around the world on continents and the ocean floors, are commonly sites of volcanic and earthquake activity. (For further information, see the **Fault** chapter.)

Forces and changes: Construction and destruction

The dominant agent of erosion on the surface of the planet is flowing water. Although the ice in glaciers is solid, it also flows (though more slowly than water in a stream channel). Both streams and glaciers move downhill under the influence of gravity, the main driving force behind almost all agents of erosion. As they move downward, they transport sediment they have picked up or that has fallen into or onto them.

Stream erosion

The shaping of stream valleys is due to a combination of erosion by flowing water and mass wasting, the spontaneous movement of Earth material down a slope in response to gravity. This does not include material transported downward by streams, winds, or glaciers. Through mass wasting, material from higher elevations is moved to lower elevations where streams, glaciers, and wind pick it up and move it to even lower elevations. Mass wasting occurs continuously on all slopes. While some mass-wasting processes act very slowly, others occur very suddenly. The general term landslide is used to describe all relatively rapid forms of mass wasting. (For further information, see the **Landslide and other gravity movements** chapter.)

Once a stream forms, it seeks out its base level, which is the level below which the stream cannot erode. Base level is the elevation of the large body of water, such as a lake or ocean, into which a stream drains. The general or ultimate base level for most larger streams is sea level. For

a tributary, base level is the point where it empties into a larger stream. Aided by gravity, a stream tries to reach its base level as quickly as possible. The larger the difference in height between the stream and its base level, the greater the erosive or cutting force of the stream. Temporary base levels may form along a stream's course, such as those created by a lake or resistant rock.

The resistance of the rock over which a stream flows determines the shape of its initial stream valley. In a highland area, a stream's erosional force is directed along its bed, not its banks, as it seeks to lower its channel to base level. If the rock over which the stream flows in this area is hard and resistant to erosion, the stream will cut a narrow, steep-walled canyon. The valley created exists as a nearly vertical notch with no floor. If the rock is less resistant to erosion, the stream will still downcut, but the sides of the valley will take on the characteristic V shape as mass wasting—rockfalls and other types of landslides—widens the upper portion of the valley.

Rock hardness is an important factor in erosion, but a stream's ability to cut depends on how much sediment it carries and how fast it is flowing. The sediment carried by a stream may have been eroded from the bed and banks

The glacier-carved crescent-shaped Hunza Valley in Pakistan.
PHOTOGRAPH REPRODUCED BY PERMISSION OF THE CORBIS CORPORATION.

of the stream, or it may have fallen into the stream after a mass-wasting event moved it down a slope bordering the stream's channel. Water moving at a low velocity or speed can move only small, fine particles such as sand, silt, and clay. Water moving at a high velocity can move a larger amount of both small particles and large, coarse particles such as boulders. Water that flows erratically, giving rise to swirls and eddies, is said to be turbulent, and turbulent water can move the coarsest and greatest amount of particles.

A stream erodes through hydraulic action and abrasion. Hydraulic action is the force exerted by the water itself. This force works along the banks of streams, attacking and undermining layers of soil and rock. Abrasion is the grinding and scraping of the stream's banks and bed by the sediment carried by the stream.

When a stream flows out of a highland area, reaching an elevation that is closer to its base level, it begins to slow down. In this state, the stream is still eroding downward, but its main force of erosion is directly laterally or horizontally against its banks. It begins meandering, winding back and forth, carving out a valley floor between valley walls or bluffs. Periodically, the stream will flood all or a part of its valley, depositing sediment on its developing floodplain.

At the lower reaches of a stream, where it approaches base level, the valley it flows through will be open, wide, and flat-bottomed. Valley walls, if they even exist, will be far away from the stream channel.

Glacial erosion

Moving glaciers not only transport material as they move, they also sculpt and carve away the land beneath them. A glacier's weight, combined with its gradual movement, can drastically reshape the landscape.

A valley glacier moves to lower elevations under the force of gravity through a combination of internal flow and sliding at its base. The ice in a glacier is so dense and under such pressure that it begins to behave like a thick tar, flowing outward and downward. Glacial movement through this internal flow is very slow. On average, it measures only an inch or two (a few centimeters) a day. In a valley glacier, ice in the upper central part moves faster than ice at the sides, where it is in contact with the valley walls. The considerable weight of a valley glacier also creates enormous pressure at its base, and this pressure lowers the temperature at which ice melts. A layer of water develops between the glacial ice and the ground. The water reduces friction by lubricating the ground and allowing the glacier to slide on its bed.

A valley glacier is capable of eroding and transporting huge amounts of sediment. As the glacier moves, its ice flows into and refreezes in fractures in the rock walls and floor of the valley. The glacier then plucks that rocky material away with it, some of which may be boulders the size of houses. This

material then becomes embedded in the ice at the base and along the sides of the glacier. As the glacier continues to move, the embedded material abrades or scrapes the rock surrounding the glacier like a giant file.

Following an existing V-shaped valley, a glacier erodes the valley, deepening and widening it. It may increase the width of the valley by as much as tens of miles (kilometers). The glacier also flattens the valley floor because ice tends to cut down over a wider area than flowing water. When the glacier finally retreats, a thick layer of glacial sediment called ground moraine remains, filling in any irregularities in the valley floor.

The 150-mile-long Shenandoah Valley in northern Virginia. **PHOTOGRAPH REPRODUCED BY PERMISSION OF THE CORBIS CORPORATION.**

Spotlight on famous forms

Napa Valley, California

California's Napa Valley is world-renowned for having a wide variety of soils and climate conditions that help produce grapes that are made into quality wines. The narrow valley is 30 miles (48 kilometers) long and 1 to

6 miles (1.6 to 9.6 kilometers) wide. It occupies an area of about 300,000 acres (120,000 hectares).

At its northern end lies the region's largest mountain, Mount St. Helena. Its southern end opens to San Pablo Bay, an arm of the San Francisco Bay system. The valley is bordered by two mountain ranges, the Vaca Mountains on the east and the Macayamas Mountains on the west. Flowing through the middle of this valley is the 50-mile-long (80-kilometer-long) Napa River.

The valley began to form about four million years ago when heat forces beneath Earth's crust in this region forced land on either side of the present-day valley upward into mountains. Certain areas between the mountains were widened and lowered into troughs as a result. Napa Valley is such an area. After the valley's formation, eruptions from several volcanoes surrounding the valley blanketed the land in volcanic cinders and ash that accumulated to layers thousands of feet thick.

Shenandoah Valley, Virginia

The Shenandoah Valley in northern Virginia is part of the Great Valley of the Appalachians, which stretches from Pennsylvania to Alabama. The Shenandoah Valley, which is about 150 miles (241 kilometers) long, lies between the Blue Ridge Mountains on the east and the Allegheny Mountains on the west.

Both mountain ranges are part of the Appalachian Mountain system, which formed over 300 million years ago. The powerful erosive forces of water, wind, and frost have greatly eroded the Appalachians since then. Water runoff has carved the mountains' distinctive alternating pattern of ridges and valleys.

The Shenandoah River, which runs through the valley, is a tributary of the Potomac River. It was the first of the tributaries in the area to reach the soft limestone layer that is now the base of the Shenandoah Valley. Intercepting stream after stream west of the Blue Ridge Mountains, the Shenandoah River grew. As it did, it carved out the Shenandoah Valley, dissolving the limestone and carrying the sediments north to the Potomac.

Yosemite Valley, California

Lying in the Sierra Nevada Mountains in central California is a 0.5-mile (0.8-kilometer) deep depression. Measuring 7 miles (11 kilometers) long and 1 mile (1.6 kilometers) wide, Yosemite Valley lies at the heart of Yosemite National Park, which encompasses 761,170 acres (304,468 hectares).

The Merced River runs through the valley. Geologists estimate that a few million years ago, it began to carve a valley where the present-day

Yosemite Valley lies. The Sierra Nevada Mountains were uplifted and tilted westward, causing the river to gradually, then rapidly, erode a deep, steep-walled canyon. About 2 million years ago, North America's climate began to cool and glaciers began to form. During one of the major glacial periods, about 700,000 years ago, ice thickness in the area was up to 6,000 feet (1,829 meters). Massive, flowing glacial ice caused tremendous amounts of rock to be carved and transported to the area, creating massive rock formations that still exist.

The flow and retreat of glaciers through Yosemite Valley occurred many times until about 10,000 years ago, when the last major glacial period ended in North America. What remained was a U-shaped valley that was actually deeper than the present-day Yosemite Valley. Rock debris from the glacier had dammed the valley creating ancient Lake Yosemite, which covered the valley floor. Streams from hanging valleys above fell in towering waterfalls. The tallest of these is Yosemite Falls, which presently drops 2,425 feet (739 meters) to the valley floor. Ultimately, sediment filled in the lake until it formed the existing valley floor.

Yosemite Valley, seven miles long and one mile across, was formed during six key geologic stages that occurred over millions of years. **PHOTOGRAPH REPRODUCED BY PERMISSION OF THE CORBIS CORPORATION.**

For More Information

Books

Huber, N. King. *The Geologic Story of Yosemite National Park*. Washington, D.C.: U.S. Geological Survey, 1987.

Web Sites

"A Glacier Carves a U-Shaped Valley." *U.S. Geological Survey and the National Park Service*. http://wrgis.wr.usgs.gov/docs/parks/glacier/uvalley.html (accessed on August 14, 2003).

"Valley and Stream Erosion." *Bryant Watershed Project*. http://www.watersheds.org/earth/valley.htm (accessed on August 14, 2003).

Valley Glaciers. http://www.zephryus.demon.co.uk/geography/resources/glaciers/valley.html (accessed on August 14, 2003).

Volcano

Volcanoes are landforms whose shapes may remain unchanged for centuries or may change drastically in minutes. Some exist singly, looming over a flat landscape. Others exist in groups, forming mountain ranges. Scores of volcanoes remain unseen, hidden beneath the surface of the planet's oceans. These submarine volcanoes are known as seamounts. (For further information on oceanic landforms, see the **Ocean basin** chapter.)

The material and processes deep within Earth that form volcanoes have shaped the planet's surface since its beginning more than four billion years ago. Volcanologists, scientists who study volcanoes and volcanic phenomena, have identified the existence of more than forty thousand volcanoes on Earth. Currently, there are about six hundred active volcanoes scattered around the world. Volcanologists classify an active volcano as one that has erupted in the last few hundred years or shows signs of erupting in the near future. A dormant volcano is one that has not erupted for a few hundred years, but has erupted in the last few thousand years. An extinct volcano is one that has not erupted in the last few thousand years and will not, volcanologists believe, ever erupt again.

The word volcano comes from the name of the Roman god of fire and a small island that is part of a group of volcanic islands located just north of Sicily in the Tyrrhenian Sea. Ancient Romans believed that Vulcan, the mythological god who made tools and weapons for other Roman gods, operated his forge beneath the island of Vulcano. One of the present-day Aeolian (pronounced ee-OH-lee-an) Islands, Vulcano has been volcanically active for thousands of years. During the Middle Ages in Western Europe (roughly from 500 to 1500 C.E.), many people considered the smoking crater on Vulcano to be the entrance to hell. After this period, the word volcano was applied to all such eruptive landforms.

The shape of the land

Technically, a volcano is a vent or hole in Earth's surface through which heated material escapes from underground. That material could be any combination of magma (called lava once it reaches Earth's surface), rock fragments, ash, and gas. Ejected through the vent, volcanic material accumulates to form a hill or, if over 1,000 feet (305 meters), a mountain around the opening. It is this accumulating landform that is more commonly referred to as a volcano.

Volcanologists recognize various volcanic landforms, such as shield volcanoes, stratovolcanoes, cinder cones, lava domes, calderas, and lava plateaus. The differing shapes of these landforms are determined by the composition of the magma flowing into the specific volcano from underground.

Magma is molten (melted) rock that contains particles of mineral grains and dissolved gas (primarily water vapor and carbon dioxide). The most abundant element found in magma is silicon, in the form of the oxide silica. (An oxide is a compound of an element and oxygen. As magma cools, the silica crystallizes to become the mineral quartz.) The

The world's highest active volcano, Mount Cotopaxi, rises 19,388 feet above the surrounding highland plain in central Ecuador. Mount Cotopaxi is a stratovolcano with an almost perfectly symmetrical cone. **PHOTOGRAPH REPRODUCED BY PERMISSION OF THE CORBIS CORPORATION.**

Words to Know

Asthenosphere: The section of the mantle immediately beneath the lithosphere that is composed of partially melted rock.

Basalt: A dark, dense volcanic rock, about 50 percent of which is silica.

Convection current: The circular movement of a gas or liquid between hot and cold areas.

Crust: The thin, solid outermost layer of Earth.

Hot spot: An area beneath Earth's crust where magma currents rise.

Lava: Magma that has reached Earth's surface.

Lithosphere: The rigid uppermost section of the mantle combined with the crust.

Magma: Molten rock containing particles of mineral grains and dissolved gas that forms deep within Earth.

Magma chamber: A reservoir or cavity beneath Earth's surface containing magma that feeds a volcano.

Mantle: The thick, dense layer of rock that lies beneath Earth's crust.

Mountain: A landmass that rises 1,000 feet (305 meters) or more above its surroundings and has steep sides meeting in a summit that is much narrower in width than the base of the landmass.

Plates: Large sections of Earth's lithosphere that are separated by deep fault zones.

Plate tectonics: The geologic theory that Earth's crust is composed of rigid plates that "float" toward or away from each other, either directly or indirectly, shifting continents, forming mountains and new ocean crust, and stimulating volcanic eruptions.

Pyroclastic material: Rock fragments, crystals, ash, pumice, and glass shards formed by a volcanic explosion or ejection from a volcanic vent.

Ring of Fire: The name given to the geographically active belt around the Pacific Ocean that is home to more than 75 percent of the planet's volcanoes.

Silica: An oxide (a compound of an element and oxygen) found in magma that, when cooled, crystallizes to become the mineral quartz, which is one of the most common compounds found in Earth's crust.

Subduction zone: A region where two plates come together and the edge of one plate slides beneath the other.

Viscosity: The measure of a fluid's resistance to flow.

amount of silica in magma determines how easily the magma flows. When discussing the flow rate of magma, volcanologists refer to its viscosity (pronounced vis-KOS-eh-tee), which is the measure of a fluid's resistance to flow. If a fluid is thin and runny, like water, it has a low viscosity or is less viscous (pronounced VIS-kus). If a fluid is thick and slow-moving, like tar, then it has a high viscosity or is more viscous. Magma's viscosity is directly related to its silica content: The higher the silica content, the higher the viscosity and the slower it flows. Temperature and the amount of gas contained in magma also affect its viscosity, but opposite that of silica. When its temperature is high and it contains a vast amount of dissolved gas, magma has a low viscosity and flows quite readily.

Lava (magma that has erupted from a volcano) can create interesting rock formations once it has run down the side of a volcano and cooled. Two such formations generated by lava flows include aa (pronounced AH-ah) and pahoehoe (pronounced pa-HOY-hoy), which are quite common in the Hawaiian Islands. In fact, about 99 percent of the island of Hawaii is composed of aa and pahoehoe. The different textures of these volcanic rocks are caused by a difference in the viscosity of the lava flows that created them. Slow-moving, cooler, and more viscous lava hardens to form aa, rough blocks that have sharp, jagged edges. Lava flows that are hotter, have a high concentration of gas, and are less viscous harden to form pahoehoe, which has a smooth, coiled surface that resembles rope. While a hard skin develops on the surface of pahoehoe as it cools, hot lava continues to flow beneath the skin, causing the coiled-rope wrinkles that mark its surface. Lava may continue to flow inside hardened pahoehoe for miles.

Shield volcano

Shield volcanoes are broad landforms with gently sloping sides, resembling a warrior's shield lying on the ground with the curved face up. These types of volcanoes are typically created by successive nonexplosive eruptions of lava that have low silica content and, consequently, relatively low viscosity. The runny lava flows great distances over the wide surface of the volcano, forming thin sheets of nearly uniform thickness. The slope of a shield volcano is seldom more than 10 degrees at its summit and 2 degrees at its base. Hawaii, Tahiti, Samoa, the Galápagos, and many other oceanic islands are actually the upper portions of large shield volcanoes.

Stratovolcano

Stratovolcanoes, also called composite volcanoes, have the most symmetrical cone shape of any volcano types. They are among the most picturesque landforms on Earth. These steep mountains have slopes of up to 30 degrees at the summit, tapering off to 5 degrees at the base. They are built up of alternating layers of lava and layers of pyroclastic (pronounced pie-row-KLAS-tic; fragmented rock, crystals, ash, pumice, and glass shards) material, which have flowed down on different sides of the volcano at different times. The steep slope near the summit is due partly to thick, viscous lava flows that did not travel far downward from the vent. The gentler slope near the base is due to the accumulation of pyroclastic material that the volcano erupted violently and material eroded from the sides of the volcano. Examples of stratovolcanoes include Mount Fuji in Japan, Mount Mayon in the Philippines, and Mount Vesuvius in Italy. In the United States, Mount Rainier and Mount Baker in Washington and Mount Hood in Oregon are classic examples of stratovolcanoes.

The twisted, ropelike texture of pahoehoe. Pahoehoe is formed when a hard skin develops on the surface of lava, while hot lava continues to flow underneath. **PHOTOGRAPH REPRODUCED BY PERMISSION OF THE CORBIS CORPORATION.**

Cinder cone

Cinder cones are the steepest of volcanoes, with slopes of 30 to 40 degrees. They are seldom taller than 1,640 feet (500 meters); many are not more than a few hundred feet high. Cinder cones are built entirely or almost entirely of blobs of lava that have broken up into small fragments

Cross-section of an active volcano.

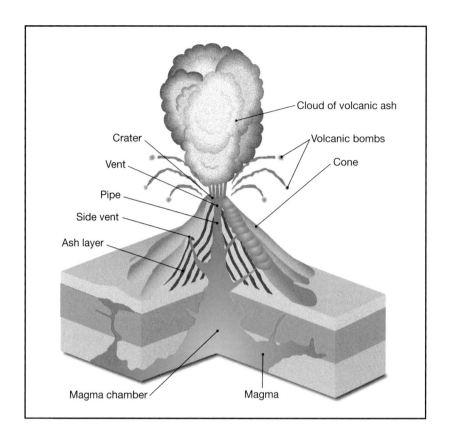

Cloud of volcanic ash

Crater

Volcanic bombs

Vent

Cone

Pipe

Side vent

Ash layer

Magma chamber

Magma

or cinders after being ejected in mildly explosive eruptions. The cinders rain back down to form a cone around a bowl-shaped depression or crater at the summit. These volcanoes can grow very rapidly, but they are usually not active for long. Because the material that forms them is fragmented and easily eroded, cinder cones usually do not remain as landforms for an extended period of time. All cinder cones currently on Earth originated within the last 1 to 2 million years; most are less than 150,000 years old. Sunset Crater in Arizona, Stromboli in the Mediterranean Sea, Parícutin in Mexico, and Cerro Negro in Nicaragua are all examples of cinder cones.

Lava dome

Lava domes, also called volcanic domes, form in the craters of volcanoes (mostly stratovolcanoes) after a major eruption. Highly viscous lava with little gas content oozes out of the volcano's vent like toothpaste out of a tube. The pasty lava is too thick to flow, and it solidifies on top of the vent, forming a rounded, steep-sided mound. The building of lava domes can be a forceful process, with small but violent explosions blasting out pieces of the dome. Fresh viscous lava flows then replace and build on the old material, causing the dome to take on a variety of strange shapes. Examples of lava domes include Mono Dome in California and Santiaguito Dome in Guatemala. After Mount St. Helens in the state of Washington erupted in May 1980, a lava dome began to form in its crater. Currently, the dome rises more than 900 feet (275 meters) above the crater floor.

Caldera

Below the vent in a volcano is a passageway called a pipe. The pipe leads down to the magma chamber, a large area where magma collects below Earth's surface. In some highly explosive eruptions, a great percentage or all of a volcano's magma chamber may be emptied. When this occurs, the roof of the magma chamber may be left unsupported. It may then collapse under its own weight, forming a large, usually circular, steepwalled basin known as a caldera (Spanish for cauldron or kettle) across the top of the volcano. Calderas have a diameter ranging from 1 to 15 miles (1.6 to 25 kilometers). Over time, rain and snowmelt may collect in a caldera, forming a lake. Lake Toba, in Sumatra, Indonesia, fills the world's largest caldera. It measures 18.6 miles (30 kilometers) wide and 62 miles (100 kilometers) long. The central part of Yellowstone National Park in Wyoming is a caldera measuring 28 miles (45 kilometers) by 47 miles (75 kilometers). A huge eruption 600,000 years ago created the depression at the heart of the park.

Lava plateau

In some eruptions, lava pours forth through fissures or long, narrow cracks in the ground instead of through a central vent in a volcano. This thin lava tends to spread out rapidly and widely, flooding the surrounding landscape. Repeated outpourings of lava eventually build up to create flat lava plains called lava plateaus. Lava plateaus are also known as flood basalts, after the dark, dense volcanic rock called basalt that floods across the surface of the land. Although erupted in thin sheets, the lava flows accumulate to form deposits thousands of feet thick.

The most famous example of a lava plateau in the United States is the Columbia Plateau, covering most of southern Washington from its border with Idaho west to the Pacific Ocean and extending south into Oregon. In places, it measures 5,000 feet (1,524 meters) thick. The Deccan Plateau of west-central India is much larger, covering some 300,000 square miles (770,000 square kilometers) and accumulating in spots to a thickness of 6,000 feet (1,829 meters). Larger still is the Siberian Traps in central Russia, which formed about 250 million years ago. It covers about 750,000 square miles (1,942,500 square kilometers). If the lava that poured forth

A Venutian Volcano on Earth?

The only active volcano in the East African Rift Valley in northern Tanzania, Ol Doinyo Lengai (pronounced ol DOYN-yo LEN-guy) rises 9,479 feet (2,890 meters). Its name means "Mountain of God" in the language of the Masai people who inhabit this region. What makes the stratovolcano so strange and interesting to volcanologists and other scientists is the lava it erupts.

While most of the world's volcanoes erupt silicate lavas, which are made up primarily of silicon and oxygen, Ol Doinyo Lengai erupts a lava rich in calcium and sodium. Volcanologists call this type of lava natrocarbonatite, and it is erupted from no other active volcano on Earth. At about 950°F (510°C), natrocarbonatite lava is approximately one-half as hot as normal lava. It is also the most fluid lava in the world. With a very low gas content, it has a very low viscosity and flows like water.

Since it is not as hot as normal lava, natrocarbonatite lava does not glow as brightly. In sunlight, lava flows from Ol Doinyo Lengai may be mistaken for dark brown or black mudflows. The dark lava quickly solidifies, then changes color to gray. When it comes in contact with moisture, the lava undergoes a chemical reaction that turns it white. This change may occur immediately if it is raining or may take several months in dry conditions. The reaction to moisture also softens the lava, so a person walking on it may sink in slightly.

Ol Doinyo Lengai is unique on Earth, but not in the solar system. Scientists have discovered through satellite photos that similar volcanic structures and lava flows exist on the planet Venus.

to create the Siberian Traps were spread out evenly across the entire planet, it would create a layer 10 feet (3 meters) thick.

Forces and changes: Construction and destruction

A volcanic eruption is among the most powerful forces on Earth. When Mount St. Helens in the state of Washington erupted in May 1980, the energy it released was equivalent to the largest hydrogen bomb ever exploded (a hydrogen bomb equals the power of one thousand atomic bombs). The eruption of the ancient volcano that produced Crater Lake in Oregon, one of the best-known calderas in the world, was forty-two times as powerful as that of Mount St. Helens. One hundred times more powerful was the 1815 eruption of the stratovolcano Tambora on the Indonesian island of Sumbawa. The ash cloud released by the volcano lowered global temperatures by as much as 5°F (3°C) from late spring to early autumn the following year. Subsequent crop failures produced widespread famine.

Ol Doinyo Lengai volcano, Tanzania. **PHOTOGRAPH REPRODUCED BY PERMISSION OF THE CORBIS CORPORATION.**

Earth's interior

The power to change the shape both of a volcano and the landscape around it comes from miles beneath Earth's surface. The interior of the planet is divided into different layers of varying composition. The rocky outer layer that forms Earth's surface is the crust, which varies in thickness from 3 to 31 miles (5 to 50 kilometers). The crust is thickest below land and thinnest below the oceans. Underlying the crust is a thick layer of rocks (different from those composing the crust) known as the mantle. The mantle extends down roughly 1,800 miles (2,900 kilometers) beneath the planet's surface.

The uppermost section of the mantle is a rigid or firm layer. Combined with the overlying solid crust, it makes up the lithosphere (pronounced LITH-uh-sfeer; from the Greek word *lithos*, meaning "stone"). On average, the lithosphere measures about 60 miles (100 kilometers) thick. The part of the mantle immediately beneath the rigid, cold lithosphere is composed of partially melted rock that is pliable, like putty. This

Cultural Landforms

According to Navajo legend, on a towering landform in what is now northwestern New Mexico, a battle took place between a warrior and monster birds that had been terrorizing the ancestors of the Navajo people. Because the warrior was victorious, the Navajo were able to settle in this area around the landform they came to call Tsé Bit'a'i (pronounced say bid-ah-ih; meaning "rock with wings"). When European settlers arrived centuries later, they thought the landform the Navajo held sacred looked like a giant sailing ship, and so they called it Shiprock.

Shiprock is located in the four corners area of America's Southwest, the only spot where four states (Utah, Colorado, Arizona, and New Mexico) meet. An area of sandstone cliffs and rugged mountains, it is the traditional homeland of several Native American tribes. Shiprock sits in the middle of what volcanologists call the Navajo volcanic field. It is littered with the remains of dozens of extinct volcanoes that last erupted twenty-five to thirty million years ago.

Shiprock stands 1,969 feet (600 meters) above the surrounding plain and measures 1,640 feet (500 meters) in diameter at its greatest width. It is a spectacular example of a volcanic neck or plug. When a volcano stops erupting and becomes extinct, remaining magma and other volcanic material may harden in the volcano's pipe, the passageway between the magma chamber and the vent. Typically, this material tends to be more resistant to erosion than the enclosing volcanic landform. Thus, long after the volcano has eroded away, the volcanic neck stands out against the landscape as the fossil remains of a once great volcano.

Volcanologists estimate that the summit of the original volcano stood almost 1,000 feet (305 meters) above Shiprock's current height. Radiating out from the volcanic neck into the flat, eroded plain are six long, thin, wall-like structures, the ancient volcano's only other visible remains. These vertical structures, called dikes, were created when magma pushed up through cracks that formed in the rock layers beneath the volcano. The rock layers have long since eroded away, leaving the dikes above the surface. The dikes range in length from 0.6 to 5.5 miles (1 to 9 kilometers).

section, called the asthenosphere (pronounced as-THEN-uh-sfeer; from the Greek word *asthenes*, meaning "weak"), extends to a depth of about 155 miles (250 kilometers).

Beneath the mantle is Earth's core, which is composed of a solid inner portion and a liquid outer portion. Both layers of the core are made of the metal elements iron and nickel. Scientists believe temperatures in the core exceed 9,900°F (5,482°C). If the heat energy created by such high

Shiprock is an eroded volcano plume, or volcanic neck, that stands more than 1,900 feet from the desert plain in New Mexico. **PHOTOGRAPH REPRODUCED BY PERMISSION OF THE CORBIS CORPORATION.**

temperatures were not released, Earth would become so hot its entire interior would melt. This energy is carried to the surface of the planet by convection currents, the circular movement of molten material deep within Earth.

When a gas or liquid is heated, it expands and becomes less dense (or lighter). It then rises above cooler, denser gas or liquid that surrounds it. This action takes place in Earth's mantle. Under tremendous pressure and

Volcano Facts

- There are 224 volcanoes located in the continental United States and Alaska. About half of them are located in Alaska alone.

- The ash cloud from a volcanic eruption can produce lightning. Collisions between the rapidly moving ash particles produce electric charges, which build up until they discharge to form a lightning bolt.

- The most active volcano in the United States is Kilauea (pronounced kee-low-AY-ah) on the island of Hawaii. Kilauea has been erupting nearly continuously since 1983.

- Stromboli, one of the Aeolian Islands of Italy, has been erupting almost continuously with relatively small explosions and occasional bigger explosions and lava flows for the last 2,000 years.

- The first volcanic eruption ever to be described in detail was that of Mount Vesuvius, which erupted in 79 C.E. and buried the Roman cities of Pompeii and Herculaneum. Pliny the Younger, who witnessed the eruption from a distance of 18 miles (29 kilometers), wrote down his observations afterward.

- Volcanologists estimate that fifteen to twenty volcanoes are erupting around the world at any given moment.

- The 1883 eruption of Krakatau in Indonesia created a tsunami (pronounced tsoo-NAH-mee; a series of great ocean waves caused by a large displacement of water) greater than 115 feet (35 meters) in height that drowned an estimated 36,000 people. The volcanic explosion was heard almost 3,000 miles (4,827 kilometers) away.

- The most common elements in materials erupted by volcanoes are silicon, oxygen, magnesium, iron, aluminum, calcium, sodium, potassium, titanium, phosphorous, carbon, hydrogen, and sulfur.

- The fastest recorded speed of a lava flow was about 37 miles (60 kilometers) per hour at Nyiragongo volcano in Zaire.

- The temperature of basalt, the hottest type of lava, can reach almost 2,150°F (1,200°C).

high temperature, mantle rock near the core heats up and expands. This makes it less dense and more buoyant, and it slowly rises to the surface. Near the surface, the hot rock moves sideways along the underside of the lithosphere, losing its heat. As it cools, the rock becomes denser, or heavier, and sinks back toward the core, only to be heated once again. This continuous motion of heated material rising, cooling, and sinking within Earth's mantle forms circular currents: convection currents. The time involved for heated rocks to rise from the lower mantle to the surface, cool, and return to the interior is estimated to be around 200 million years.

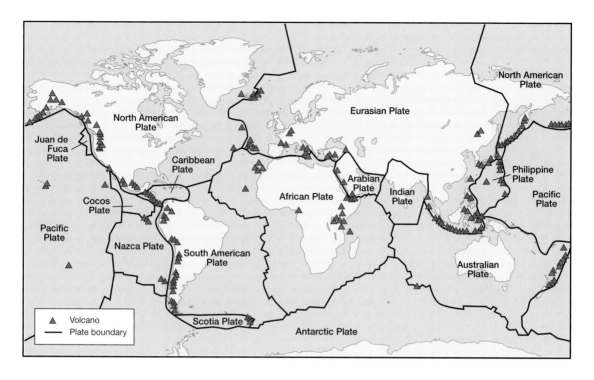

Plate tectonics

The slowly moving convection currents are able to release their heat energy near the surface of the planet because both Earth's interior and its surface are in motion. Earth's lithosphere is not solid, but is broken into many large slabs or plates that "float" on the hot, soft asthenosphere. There are seven large plates, eight medium-sized plates, and a number of smaller ones. These plates are in constant contact with each other, fitting together like a jigsaw puzzle. When one plate moves, it causes other plates to move. The movement of the plates toward or away from each other is in response to the pressure exerted by the convection currents. Scientists used the word tectonics (from the Greek word *tekton*, meaning "builder") to describe the movements. The scientific theory explaining the plates and their movements and interactions is known as plate tectonics.

The major geologic features of Earth, from volcanoes to mountains to basins to oceanic trenches, are all the result of plate movement. Plates move at rates from about 1 to 6 inches (2.5 to 15 centimeters) per year. The plates interact with each other in one of three ways: they move toward each other (converge), they move away from each other (diverge), or they slide past each other (transform). The boundaries where plates meet and interact are known as plate margins.

Map of the active volcanoes around the world. Notice how the majority of volcanoes exist along the plate margins.

Walking in the Footsteps of Giants

It is called the Giant's Causeway: a mass of closely packed lava columns whose tops seem to form stepping stones that lead from a cliff along the coast of Northern Ireland and disappear under the North Channel. There are approximately forty thousand of these columns, most of which are roughly hexagonal (six-sided) in shape. The rest have between four and eight sides. The tallest columns stand 40 feet (12 meters) high, and the hardened lava in the cliff is 90 feet (27 meters) thick in places.

A causeway is a raised path or road over water or across land that is sometimes covered by water. The ancient Irish believed that a giant created this landform for such a purpose. According to legend, Finn MacCool (Fionn mac Cumhail is the Gaelic spelling of his name) was a warrior and commander of the armies of the kingdom of Ireland. One day, his fighting abilities were questioned by Benendoner, a Scottish giant. MacCool then challenged the giant, but Benendoner could not swim and so was not able to come to

Ireland to answer the challenge. Enraged, MacCool used his sword to cut sections from the cliff, which he then threw into the channel between Ireland and Scotland to create the causeway so the two giants could meet to settle their dispute.

Scientists have known since the late eighteenth century that lava flows formed the strange columns, but the cause behind their regular geometric shape remained a mystery until the twentieth century. Scientists now know that the volcanic rock in the area is made of basalt, which flowed smoothly out of fissures or cracks in Earth's surface about sixty million years ago. As basalt cools, it shrinks. The basalt that formed the causeway, however, did not cool slowly and shrink evenly. Scientists believe water most likely may have washed over it, accelerating its cooling. As the basalt cooled rapidly, randomly scattered areas across its surface cooled before other areas. The stress of the rapid cooling and uneven shrinking would have caused cracks to form along the surface and continue downward, much in the same way that mud dries in a puddle of water that has evaporated.

There are three types of convergent plate margins or areas where two plates move toward each other: continental-continental, continental-oceanic, and oceanic-oceanic. When two continental (land) plates converge, they crumple up and compress, forming complex mountain ranges of great height. The rocks making up oceanic crust are denser (heavier) than those making up continental crust. So when an oceanic plate converges with another plate, either continental or oceanic, it slides beneath the other. The region where this occurs is

The basalt columns of Giant's Causeway on the coast of Northern Ireland. Scientists believe the strange for-mation was created when an ancient lava flow quickly cooled and solidified. **PHOTOGRAPH REPRODUCED BY PERMIS-SION OF THE CORBIS CORPORATION.**

known as the subduction zone, and this is where most of the world's explosive volcanoes form.

When an oceanic plate subducts, or sinks, beneath a continental plate, the leading edge of the oceanic plate is pushed farther and farther beneath the continent's surface. When it reaches about 70 miles (112 kilometers) into the mantle, high temperature and pressure melt the rock at the edge of the plate, forming thick, flowing magma. Since magma is less dense than the rock that typically surrounds it deep underground, the magma tends to rise toward Earth's surface. Driven by pressure created by gas bubbles within it, the magma forces its way through weakened layers of rock to collect in underground reservoirs called magma chambers.

As magma rises through the mantle to Earth's surface, the surrounding pressure on it decreases, allowing the magma to expand. As more and more magma collects in a magma chamber, pressure from the expanding magma increases until it exceeds that of the overlying rock. An explosion then occurs, and the magma is forced out of the chamber upward through cracks or vents in the planet's surface. The severity of the explosion is dependent on the composition of the magma. If it has a low viscosity, its gases can escape rapidly, and it flows rather than exploding. If it has a high viscosity, its gases cannot escape as quickly. Pressure builds until the gases escape violently in an explosion.

Ring of Fire

Volcanoes are not scattered widely across the surface of Earth. Most are concentrated on the edges of continents, along island chains, or beneath the sea forming long mountain ranges. A majority of the world's active volcanoes above sea level are located in a geographic belt called the Ring of Fire. This belt encompasses the lands on the edges of the Pacific Ocean. It also marks the boundary where the Pacific Plate subducts beneath the plates surrounding it. The Ring of Fire follows the west coast of the Americas from Chile to Alaska. It runs through the Andes Mountains, Central America, Mexico, California, the Cascade Mountains, and the Aleutian Islands. It continues down the east coast of Asia from Siberia to New Zealand, through Kamchatka, the Kurile Islands, Japan, the Philippines, Celebes, New Guinea, the Solomon Islands, and New Caledonia.

Since a vast percentage of all magma reaching Earth's surface does so under the oceans, most of the planet's volcanoes are located there. Some protrude above the water as islands; others lie entirely beneath the surface. Most form along mid-ocean ridges, which are long, narrow structures where oceanic plates are diverging or moving apart and magma rises to fill the gap. The Mid-Atlantic Ridge, where the North and South American plates are diverging from the Eurasian and African plates, is a submerged mountain range with many volcanic features. The volcanic-rich island of Iceland lies directly over the Mid-Atlantic Ridge. (For further information on oceanic landforms, see the **Ocean basin** chapter.)

Hot spots are special areas where volcanoes form apart from plates converging or diverging, such as in the middle of the Pacific Ocean. At these places, magma rises from the mantle and erupts through Earth's crust

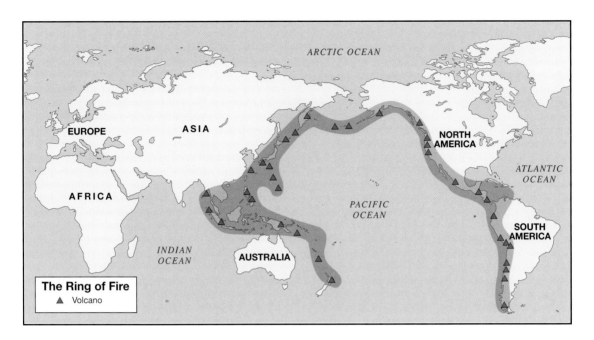

to form a volcano. Volcanologists believe these plumes of magma can exist for millions of years. A famous example of hot spot volcanoes is the string of Hawaiian islands. These islands form a chain of volcanoes because the magma plume that created them has remained stationary while the Pacific plate has shifted. As the plate moved slowly over millions of years, each volcano was cut off from its magma source and a new one formed in its place over the hot spot. The northwesternmost island in the Hawaiian chain contains the oldest rocks and is volcanically extinct; the island of Hawaii, the southeasternmost in the chain, contains the youngest rocks and is the most volcanically active of all the islands. Volcanologists believe it sits directly over the hot spot. More than one hundred hot spots have been active around the planet during the last ten million years, creating some of the world's largest volcanoes, including the present-day Hawaiian volcanoes Mauna Loa and Kilauea.

A majority of the world's active volcanoes above sea level are located in a geographic belt called the Ring of Fire.

Spotlight on famous forms
Mauna Loa, Hawaii

Mauna Loa, a very broad, flat shield volcano on the island of Hawaii, is the world's largest volcano and one of the most active. It rises 13,680 feet (4,170 meters) above sea level, and it extends more than 18,000 feet (5,544 meters) to the floor of the Pacific Ocean. From its base under the ocean to its summit, Mauna Loa measures about 32,000 feet (9,754 meters), which makes it taller than Mount Everest in the Himalayas, the

Largest Volcano in the Solar System

Olympus Mons on Mars is the largest of all known volcanoes in the solar system. It is a shield volcano that stands 16 miles (26 kilometers) high and measures 388 miles (624 kilometers) in diameter. A 4-mile-high (6-kilometer-high) scarp, or steep cliff, rims its outer edge. A caldera 50 miles (80 kilometers) wide is located at its summit. If Olympus Mons were placed on the face of Earth, it would cover an area the size of the state of Arizona.

Scientists believe Olympus Mons and other volcanoes on Mars were able to become extremely large because of two main reasons: First, there is less gravity on Mars, which allowed the volcanoes to grow without collapsing under their own weight. Second, the crust on Mars does not move as it does on Earth. This allowed lava to pile up in one large volcano instead of being distributed in an arc of volcanoes, such as the Hawaiian Islands on Earth.

Olympus Mons and all other volcanoes on Mars are extinct. Scientists estimate the youngest lava flows on the gigantic volcano are 20 to 200 million years old.

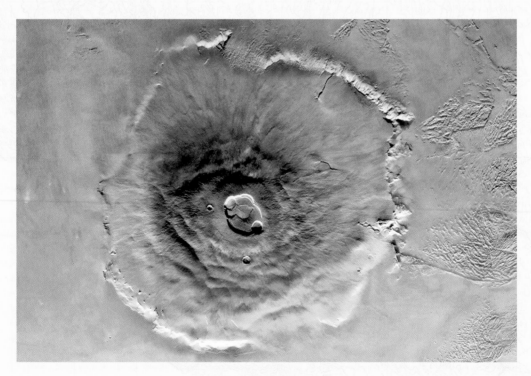

Olympus Mons, a volcano on the planet Mars. **PHOTOGRAPH REPRODUCED BY PERMISSION OF THE CORBIS CORPORATION.**

world's tallest mountain on land. The volcano, whose name means "Long Mountain" in Hawaiian, makes up just more than 50 percent of the island of Hawaii. Mauna Loa encompasses an area of about 2,035 square miles (5,271 square kilometers).

Thousands of thin flows of lava have built the volcano over hundreds of thousands of years. It currently has a volume of approximately 9,600 cubic miles (40,000 cubic kilometers). Since its first documented historical eruption in 1834, Mauna Loa has erupted thirty-three times. Its most recent eruption occurred in the spring of 1984. The lava flows it has produced in the past two centuries have covered 310 square miles (803 square kilometer).

At Mauna Loa's summit is a caldera named Mokuaweoweo (pronounced MO-koo-AH-WAI-o-WAI-o; translated literally as "fish section"). It measures 3 miles (5 kilometers) long, 1.5 miles (2.4 kilometers)

Mauna Loa, located on the island of Hawaii, is the world's largest and most active volcano. Rising 13,680 feet above sea level, the flat shield volcano encompasses an area of about 2,035 square miles, or nearly 50 percent of the entire island. **PHOTOGRAPH REPRODUCED BY PERMISSION OF THE CORBIS CORPORATION.**

wide, and 600 feet (183 meters) deep. Volcanologists believe the caldera formed 600 to 700 years ago when the volcano's magma chamber collapsed after an eruption.

Mount Cotopaxi, Ecuador

The world's highest active volcano, Mount Cotopaxi, rises 19,388 feet (5,909 meters) above the surrounding highland plain in central Ecuador. A stratovolcano with an almost perfectly symmetrical cone, Mount Cotopaxi is covered in glaciers above 14,930 feet (4,550 meters). Deep valleys are cut into its steep sides, radiating downward from its summit. The crater at its summit measures 2,625 feet (800 meters) by 2,133 feet (650 meters).

Cotopaxi, which in the local Quechua (pronounced KECH-wa) language means "neck of the Moon," has a well-recorded history of explosive eruptions. In 1534, when an invading Spanish army began an attack against the native Incas, the battle was cut short by a massive eruption. Since then, Mount Cotopaxi has erupted more than fifty times, most recently in 1904. An eruption in 1877 melted snow and ice from the summit, producing mudflows (thick mixtures of mud, water, and other surface fragments) that traveled more than 60 miles (100 kilometers) from the volcano.

Mount St. Helens, Washington

Located in southwestern Washington, Mount St. Helens is a relatively young stratovolcano, approximately forty thousand years old. Before its spectacular eruption in May of 1980, it had lain dormant since 1857. Native Americans in the area surrounding the volcano called it Louwala-Clough, meaning "smoking mountain." In the past five centuries, the volcano has produced four major eruptions and dozens of lesser ones. It is the most active volcano in the Cascade Range, a mountain chain that extends about 700 miles (1,125 kilometers) from British Columbia, Canada, to northern California.

Prior to May 18, 1980, Mount St. Helens rose to a height of 9,677 feet (2,950 meters). The fifth-tallest mountain in Washington, it had a nearly perfect cone shape, and its summit glistened in a perpetual cap of snow and ice. When the volcano exploded on that May morning in a continuous nine-hour eruption, it lost its uppermost 1,300 feet (396 meters). A massive earthquake under Mount St. Helens caused its north flank to slide away in the largest landslide in recorded history. This landslide triggered a destructive, lethal sideways blast of hot gas, steam, and rock debris that swept across the landscape as fast as 680 miles (1,095 kilometers) per hour. Within minutes of the blast, an ash plume from the destroyed crater rose 15 miles (24 kilometers) into the sky.

After the eruption, Mount St. Helens's summit stood only 8,364 feet (2,549 meters) above the destroyed landscape surrounding it—about 0.67 cubic miles (2.75 cubic kilometers) of material had been removed from the volcano. Its new horseshoe-shaped crater measured 1.2 miles (1.9 kilometers) by 1.8 miles (2.9 kilometers), and the crater floor was 2,084 feet (635 meters) deep. Within months after the main eruption, small eruptions produced thick lava that formed a lava dome in the crater. Over the next six years, subsequent eruptions generated viscous lava that added layer upon layer to the dome. At the beginning of the twenty-first century, the lava dome towered more than 900 feet (275 meters) above the crater floor.

Crater Lake, Oregon

Measuring 5 miles (8 kilometers) in diameter, Crater Lake has a surface area of 20.6 square miles (53.4 square kilometers). It is enclosed by steep rock walls that rise up almost 2,000 feet (610 meters) above its surface. With a depth of 1,943 feet (592 meters), Crater Lake is the deepest lake in the United States and the seventh-deepest in the world. No springs or other inlets feed the lake. The water that evaporates or seeps out of the lake is replaced mostly by winter snows, which average 44 feet (13.5 meters) a year.

Eruption of Mount St. Helens volcano, 1980. The volcano, located in the state of Washington, rose to a height of 9,677 feet and was a perfect cone shape before the eruption. The explosion caused the breaking away of the uppermost 1,300 feet, and resulted in the largest landslide in recorded history.

PHOTOGRAPH REPRODUCED BY PERMISSION OF THE CORBIS CORPORATION.

Crater Lake in southern Oregon is the best-known caldera in the United States. The lake measures 5 miles in diameter and has a surface area of 20.6 square miles. PHOTOGRAPH REPRODUCED BY PERMISSION OF THE CORBIS CORPORATION.

Crater Lake occupies the remains of Mount Mazama, the name given by volcanologists to this ancient cluster of overlapping stratovolcanoes that originally stood at about 12,000 feet (3,658 meters). The caldera formed when Mazama exploded violently 7,700 years ago. The eruption spewed about 18 cubic miles (75 cubic kilometers) of pyroclastic material onto thousands of square miles of surrounding landscape and caused the volcano's magma chamber to collapse. Minor eruptions afterward built a cinder cone on the floor of the caldera. Now known as Wizard Island, the cone rises 764 feet (233 meters) above the surface of the lake on its west side.

After forming, the caldera gradually filled with more than 5 trillion gallons (19 trillion liters) of water from rainfall and melting snow. The deep blue color of the lake is due to its great depth, the clarity of its water, and the way light interacts with water. Sunlight (white light) is made up of all the colors in the spectrum: red, orange, yellow, green, blue, indigo, and violet. Red light has the longest wavelength, violet the shortest. Just as a prism splits sunlight into different bands of color, so does water. As sunlight enters water, the water molecules easily absorb the longer wavelengths of light (reds, oranges, and yellows). The shorter wavelengths are more easily scattered than absorbed. Because of the depth of Crater Lake, all of the longer wavelengths of light are absorbed. Since the lake's water is so clear, the shorter wavelengths of blue and violet are able to penetrate much farther down before being scattered and redirected toward the surface. This creates what the human eye sees as an intense blue color.

For More Information

Books

Decker, Robert, and Barbara Decker. *Volcanoes*. New York: W. H. Freeman, 1997.

Morris, Neil. *Volcanoes*. New York: Crabtree Publishing, 1995.

Rosi, Mauro, Papale, Paolo, Lupi, Luca, and Marco Stoppato. *Volcanoes*. Toronto: Firefly Books, 2003.

Thompson, Luke. *Volcanoes*. New York: Children's Press, 2000.

Tilling, Robert I. *Born of Fire: Volcanoes and Igneous Rocks*. Berkeley Heights, NJ: Enslow, 1991.

Trueit, Trudy Strain. *Volcanoes*. New York: Franklin Watts, 2003.

Van Rose, Susanna. *Volcano and Earthquake*. New York: DK Publishing, 2000.

Web Sites

"Cascades Volcano Observatory: Learn About Volcanoes." *USGS*. http://vulcan.wr.usgs.gov/Outreach/AboutVolcanoes/framework.html (accessed on September 2, 2003).

The Electronic Volcano. http://www.dartmouth.edu/~volcano/ (accessed on September 2, 2003).

"Global Volcanism Program." *Smithsonian Institution*. http://www.volcano.si.edu/gvp/ (accessed on September 2, 2003).

Plate tectonics. http://www.platetectonics.com/ (accessed on September 2, 2003).

Tilling, Robert I. "Volcanoes." *USGS*. http://pubs.usgs.gov/gip/volc/ (accessed on September 2, 2003).

Volcanic Landforms. http://volcano.und.nodak.edu/vwdocs/vwlessons/landforms.html (accessed on September 2, 2003).

Volcanic Landforms of Hawaii Volcanoes National Park. http://volcano.und. nodak.edu/vwdocs/vwlessons/havo.html (accessed on September 2, 2003).

Volcano World. http://volcano.und.nodak.edu/ (accessed on September 2, 2003).

"Volcanoes of the United States." *USGS.* http://pubs.usgs.gov/gip/ volcus/ (accessed on September 2, 2003).

Where to Learn More

Books

Alvarez, Walter. *T. rex and the Crater of Doom*. Princeton: Princeton University Press, 1997.

Anderson, Peter. *A Grand Canyon Journey: Tracing Time in Stone*. New York: Franklin Watts, 1997.

Aulenbach, Nancy Holler, and Hazel A. Barton. *Exploring Caves: Journeys into the Earth*. Washington, D.C.: National Geographic, 2001.

Baars, Donald L. *A Traveler's Guide to the Geology of the Colorado Plateau*. Salt Lake City: University of Utah Press, 2002.

Barnes, F. A. *Canyon Country Geology*. Thompson Springs, UT: Arch Hunter Books, 2000.

Barnes-Svarney, Patricia L. *Born of Heat and Pressure: Mountains and Metamorphic Rocks*. Berkeley Heights, NJ: Enslow Publishers, 1999.

Beckey, Fred. *Mount McKinley: Icy Crown of North America*. Seattle, WA: Mountaineers Books, 1999.

Benn, Douglas I., and David J. A. Evans. *Glaciers and Glaciation*. London, England: Edward Arnold, 1998.

Bennett, Matthew R., and Neil F. Glasser. *Glacial Geology: Ice Sheets and Landforms*. New York: John Wiley and Sons, 1996.

Bird, Eric. *Coastal Geomorphology: An Introduction*. New York: John Wiley and Sons, 2000.

Bowen, James, and Margarita Bowen. *The Great Barrier Reef: History, Science, Heritage*. New York: Cambridge University Press, 2002.

Bridge, John S. *Rivers and Floodplains: Forms, Processes, and Sedimentary Record*. Malden, MA: Blackwell, 2002.

Brimner, Larry Dane. *Geysers*. New York: Children's Press, 2000.

Bryan, T. Scott. *The Geysers of Yellowstone*. Third ed. Boulder: University Press of Colorado, 1995.

Cerullo, Mary M. *Coral Reef: A City That Never Sleeps*. New York: Cobblehill, 1996.

Collard, Sneed B. *Lizard Island: Science and Scientists on Australia's Great Barrier Reef*. New York: Franklin Watts, 2000.

Collier, Michael. *A Land in Motion: California's San Andreas Fault*. Berkeley: University of California Press, 1999.

Davis, Richard A., Jr. *The Evolving Coast*. New York: W. H. Freeman, 1997.

Decker, Robert, and Barbara Decker. *Volcanoes*. New York: W. H. Freeman, 1997.

DenDooven, K. C. *Monument Valley: The Story Behind the Scenery*. Revised ed. Las Vegas, NV: KC Publications, 2001.

Downs, Sandra. *Earth's Fiery Fury*. Brookfield, CT: Twenty-First Century Books, 2000.

Erickson, Jon. *Glacial Geology: How Ice Shapes the Land*. New York: Facts on File, 1996.

Erickson, Jon. *Marine Geology: Exploring the New Frontiers of the Ocean*. Revised ed. New York: Facts on File, 2002.

Fisher, Richard D. *Earth's Mystical Grand Canyons*. Tucson, AZ: Sunracer Publications, 2001.

Gallant, Roy A. *Geysers: When Earth Roars*. New York: Scholastic Library Publishing, 1997.

Gallant, Roy A. *Meteorite Hunter: The Search for Siberian Meteorite Craters*. New York: McGraw-Hill, 2002.

Gallant, Roy A. *Sand on the Move: The Story of Dunes*. New York: Franklin Watts, 1997.

Gillieson, David S. *Caves: Processes, Development, and Management*. Cambridge, MA: Blackwell Publishers, 1996.

Goodwin, Peter H. *Landslides, Slumps, and Creep*. New York: Franklin Watts, 1998.

Harden, Deborah R. *California Geology*. Englewood Cliffs, NJ: Prentice Hall, 1997.

Haslett, Simon. *Coastal Systems*. New York: Routledge, 2001.

Hecht, Jeff. *Shifting Shores: Rising Seas, Retreating Coastlines*. New York: Atheneum, 1990.

Hill, Mary. *Geology of the Sierra Nevada*. Berkeley: University of California Press, 1989.

Hodge, Paul. *Meteorite Craters and Impact Structures of the Earth*. Cambridge, England: Cambridge University Press, 1994.

Hook, Cheryl. *Coral Reefs*. Philadelphia, PA: Chelsea House, 2001.

Huber, N. King. *The Geologic Story of Yosemite National Park*. Washington, D.C.: U.S. Geological Survey, 1987.

Hubler, Clark. *America's Mountains: An Exploration of Their Origins and Influences from Alaska Range to the Appalachians*. New York: Facts on File, 1995.

Jennings, Terry. *Landslides and Avalanches*. North Mankato, MN: Thameside Press, 1999.

Knox, Ray, and David Stewart. *The New Madrid Fault Finders Guide*. Marble Hill, MO: Gutenberg-Richter Publications, 1995.

Ladd, Gary. *Landforms, Heart of the Colorado Plateau: The Story Behind the Scenery*. Las Vegas, NV: KC Publications, 2001.

Lancaster, Nicholas. *The Geomorphology of Desert Dunes*. New York: Routledge, 1995.

Leopold, Luna B. *A View of the River*. Cambridge, MA: Harvard University Press, 1994.

Leopold, Luna B. *Water, Rivers and Creeks*. Sausalito, CA: University Science Books, 1997.

Llewellyn, Claire. *Glaciers*. Barrington, IL: Heinemann Library, 2000.

Mark, Kathleen. *Meteorite Craters*. Tucson: University of Arizona Press, 1987.

Martin, Linda. *Mesa Verde: The Story Behind the Scenery*. Revised ed. Las Vegas, NV: KC Publications, 2001.

Martin, Patricia A. Fink. *Rivers and Streams*. New York: Franklin Watts, 1999.

Massa, Renato. *The Coral Reef*. Translated by Linda Serio. Austin, TX: Raintree Steck-Vaughn, 1998.

McPhee, John. *Basin and Range*. New York: Farrar, Strauss, and Giroux, 1981.

Moore, George W., and Nicholas Sullivan. *Speleology: Caves and the Cave Environment*. Third ed. St. Louis, MO: Cave Books, 1997.

Morris, Neil. *Volcanoes*. New York: Crabtree Publishing, 1995.

Ollier, Cliff, and Colin Pain. *The Origin of Mountains*. New York: Routledge, 2000.

Palmer, Arthur N., and Kathleen H. Lavoie. *Introduction to Speleology*. St. Louis, MO: Cave Books, 1999.

Post, Austin, and Edward R. Lachapelle. *Glacier Ice*. Revised ed. Seattle: University of Washington Press, 2000.

Price, L. Greer. *An Introduction to Grand Canyon Geology*. Grand Canyon, AZ: Grand Canyon Association, 1999.

Rosi, Mauro, Papale, Paolo, Lupi, Luca, and Marco Stoppato. *Volcanoes*. Toronto: Firefly Books, 2003.

Rotter, Charles. *Mountains: The Towering Sentinels*. Mankato, MN: Creative Education, 2003.

Schuh, Mari C. *What Are Rivers?* Mankato, MN: Pebble Books, 2002.

Seibold, E., and W. H. Berger. *The Sea Floor*. Third ed. New York: Springer Verlag, 1996.

Sheppard, Charles. *Coral Reefs: Ecology, Threats, and Conservation*. Stillwater, MN: Voyageur Press, 2002.

Smith, Duane A. *Mesa Verde: Shadows of the Centuries*. Revised ed. Boulder: University Press of Colorado, 2003.

Steele, Duncan. *Target Earth*. Pleasantville, NY: Reader's Digest, 2000.

Tabor, Rowland, and Ralph Taugerud. *Geology of the North Cascades: A Mountain Mosaic*. Seattle, WA: Mountaineers Books, 1999.

Taylor, Michael Ray. *Caves: Exploring Hidden Realms*. Washington, D.C.: National Geographic, 2001.

Thompson, Luke. *Volcanoes*. New York: Children's Press, 2000.

Tilling, Robert I. *Born of Fire: Volcanoes and Igneous Rocks*. Berkeley Heights, NJ: Enslow, 1991.

Trimble, Stephen. *The Sagebrush Ocean: A Natural History of the Great Basin*. Reno: University of Nevada Press, 1999.

Trueit, Trudy Strain. *Volcanoes*. New York: Franklin Watts, 2003.

Vallier, Tracy. *Islands and Rapids: The Geologic Story of Hells Canyon*. Lewiston, ID: Confluence Press, 1998.

Van Rose, Susanna. *Volcano and Earthquake*. New York: DK Publishing, 2000.

Verschuur, Gerrit L. *Impact! The Threat of Comets and Asteroids*. Oxford, England: Oxford University Press, 1996.

Walker, Jane. *Avalanches and Landslides*. New York: Gloucester Press, 1992.

Wessels, Tom. *The Granite Landscape: A Natural History of America's Mountain Domes, from Acadia to Yosemite*. Woodstock, VT: Countryman Press, 2001.

Williams, David B. *A Naturalist's Guide to Canyon Country*. Helena, MT: Falcon Publishing Company, 2001.

Ylvisaker, Anne. *Landslides*. Bloomington, MN: Capstone Press, 2003.

Web sites

"About Coral Reefs." *U.S. Environmental Protection Agency.* http://www.epa.gov/owow/oceans/coral/about.html (accessed on August 14, 2003).

"All About Glaciers." *National Snow and Ice Data Center.* http://nsidc.org/glaciers/ (accessed on September 1, 2003).

"Asteroid and Comet Impact Hazards." *NASA Ames Research Center.* http://impact.arc.nasa.gov/index.html (accessed on September 1, 2003).

"Atlantic Plain Province." *U.S. Geological Survey and the National Park Service.* http://wrgis.wr.usgs.gov/docs/parks/province/atlantpl.html (accessed on August 6, 2003).

"Avalanches and Landslides." *Nearctica.* http://www.nearctica.com/geology/avalan.htm (accessed on August 27, 2003).

"Basics of Flooding." *Floodplain Management Association.* http://www.floodplain.org/flood_basics.htm (accessed on September 1, 2003).

"Basin and Coastal Morphology: Principal Features." *COAST Resource Guide.* http://www.coast-nopp.org/visualization_modules/physical_chemical/basin_coastal_morphology/principal_features/index.html (accessed on September 23, 2003).

Butte. http://geology.about.com/library/bl/images/blbutte.htm (accessed on September 1, 2003).

"Cascades Volcano Observatory: Learn About Volcanoes." *U.S. Geological Survey.* http://vulcan.wr.usgs.gov/Outreach/AboutVolcanoes/framework.html (accessed on September 2, 2003).

"Cave Facts." *American Cave Conservation Association.* http://www.cavern.org/CAVE/ACCA_index.htm (accessed on August 14, 2003).

"Caves Theme Page." *Gander Academy.* http://www.stemnet.nf.ca/CITE/cave.htm (accessed on August 14, 2003).

"Coastal and Marine Geology Program." *U.S. Geological Survey.* http://marine.usgs.gov/index.html (accessed on August 14, 2003).

Coastal Processes and the Continental Margins. http://www.ocean.washington.edu/education/magic/Ipage/happened/2/coastal.htm (accessed on September 23, 2003).

"The Coastal Scene: Oceanography from the Space Shuttle." *Goddard Space Flight Center, National Aeronautics and Space Administration.* http://daac.gsfc.nasa.gov/CAMPAIGN_DOCS/OCDST/shuttle_oceanography_web/oss_4.html (accessed on August 14, 2003).

"The Colorado Plateau: High, Wide, & Windswept." *BLM Environmental Education.* http://www.blm.gov/education/colplateau/index.html (accessed on September 2, 2003).

"Colorado Plateau Province." *U.S. Geological Survey.* http://wrgis.wr.usgs.gov/docs/parks/province/coloplat.html (accessed on August 14, 2003).

"Coral Reef Ecosystems: Tropical Rain Forest of the Sea." *Department of Geology, San Jose State University.* http://geosun1.sjsu.edu/~dreed/105/coral.html (accessed on August 14, 2003).

Coral reefs. http://www.starfish.ch/reef/reef.html (accessed on August 14, 2003).

"Coral Reefs and Associated Ecosystems." *National Oceanographic Data Center, National Oceanic and Atmospheric Administration.* http://www.nodc.noaa.gov/col/projects/coral/Coralhome.html (accessed on August 14, 2003).

"Deep Ocean Basins." *COAST Resource Guide.* http://www.coast-nopp.org/visualization_modules/physical_chemical/basin_coastal_morphology/principal_features/deep_ocean/basins.html (accessed on August 4, 2003).

"Delta." *Kent National Grid for Learning.* http://www.kented.org.uk/ngfl/rivers/River%20Articles/delta.htm (accessed on August 26, 2003).

"Deltas." *Department of Geological Sciences, Salem State College.* http://www.salem.mass.edu/~lhanson/gls214/gls214_deltas.html (accessed on August 26, 2003).

"Desert Geologic Features." *Desert USA.* http://www.desertusa.com/mag99/sep/papr/desfeatures.html (accessed on August 26, 2002).

"Deserts: Geology and Resources." *U.S. Geological Survey.* http://pubs.usgs.gov/gip/deserts/ (accessed on August 26, 2002).

"Earth Impact Database." *Planetary and Space Science Centre, University of New Brunswick.* http://www.unb.ca/passc/ImpactDatabase/ (accessed on September 1, 2003).

"Earth's Water: River and Streams." *U.S. Geological Survey.* http://ga.water.usgs.gov/edu/earthrivers.html (accessed on August 14, 2003).

Egger, Anne E. "Plate Tectonics I: The Evidence for a Geologic Revolution." *VisionLearning.* http://www.visionlearning.com/library/science/geology-1/GEO1.1-plate_tectonics_1.html (accessed on September 1, 2003).

The Electronic Volcano. http://www.dartmouth.edu/~volcano/ (accessed on September 2, 2003).

EOSC 110: Desert Photos. http://www.eos.ubc.ca/courses/eosc110/fletcher/slideshow/deserts/deserts.html (accessed on August 26, 2002).

Everest News. http://www.everestnews.com (accessed on September 1, 2003).

"Explore the Geological Wonders of South Africa—Visit the Geology of the Witwatersrand." *Geological Heritage Tours.* http://www.geosites.co.za/witsgeology.htm (accessed on August 14, 2003).

"Fault Motion." *Incorporated Research Institutions for Seismology.* http://www.iris.edu/gifs/animations/faults.htm (accessed on September 1, 2003).

"Floodplain Features and Management." *Shippensburg University.* http://www.ship.edu/~cjwolt/geology/fpl.htm (accessed on September 1, 2003).

"Floods and Flood Plains." *U.S. Geological Survey.* http://water.usgs.gov/pubs/of/ofr93-641/ (accessed on September 1, 2003).

"Ganges River Delta (image)." *Earth Observatory, NASA.* http://earthobservatory.nasa.gov/Newsroom/NewImages/images.php3?img_id=4793 (accessed on August 26, 2003).

"Geologic Hazards: Landslides." *U.S. Geological Survey.* http://landslides.usgs.gov/ (accessed on August 27, 2003).

"Geology of Fieldnotes: Mesa Verde National Park." *National Park Service.* http://www.aqd.nps.gov/grd/parks/meve/ (accessed on September 1, 2003).

Geology of Great Basin National Park. http://www.aqd.nps.gov/grd/parks/grba/ (accessed on August 14, 2003).

Geology of Rocky Mountain National Park. http://www.aqd.nps.gov/grd/parks/romo/ (accessed on September 1, 2003).

"The Geology of the Grand Canyon." *Grand Canyon Explorer.* http://www.kaibab.org/geology/gc_geol.htm (accessed on August 14, 2003).

Geology of Tibet Plateau, the Roof of the World. http://www.100gogo. com/geo.htm (accessed on September 2, 2003).

Geomorphology of the Sonoran Desert. http://alic.arid.arizona.edu/sonoran/ Physical/geomorphology.html (accessed on August 26, 2002).

"Geothermal Energy and Hydrothermal Activity: Fumaroles, Hot Springs, Geysers." *U.S. Geological Survey.* http://vulcan.wr.usgs.gov/ Glossary/ThermalActivity/description_thermal_activity.html (accessed on September 1, 2003).

The Geyser Observation and Study Association. http://www.geyserstudy.org/ (accessed on September 1, 2003).

"Geysers, Fumaroles, and Hot Springs." *U.S. Geological Survey.* http://pubs.usgs.gov/gip/volc/geysers.html (accessed on September 1, 2003).

"Glacial Landforms." *South Central Service Cooperative.* http://www.scsc. k12.ar.us/2001Outwest/PacificEcology/Projects/HendricksR/default.htm (accessed on September 1, 2003).

"A Glacier Carves a U-Shaped Valley." *U.S. Geological Survey and the National Park Service.* http://wrgis.wr.usgs.gov/docs/parks/glacier/ uvalley.html (accessed on August 14, 2003).

"Glaciers and Glacial Geology." *Montana State University-Bozeman.* http://gemini.oscs.montana.edu/~geol445/hyperglac/index.htm (accessed on September 1, 2003).

Glaciers, Rivers of Ice. http://members.aol.com/scipioiv/glmain.html (accessed on September 1, 2003).

"Global Volcanism Program." *Smithsonian Institution.* http://www.volcano. si.edu/gvp/ (accessed on September 2, 2003).

"Grand Canyon National Park: Geologic Story." *National Park Service.* http://www.nps.gov/grca/grandcanyon/quicklook/Geologicstory.htm (accessed on August 14, 2003).

"The Great Artesian Basin Information Site." *The State of Queensland Department of Natural Resources and Mines.* http://www.nrm.qld.gov. au/water/gab/ (accessed on August 14, 2003).

"The Great Plains and Prairies." *U.S. Department of State.* http://usinfo. state.gov/products/pubs/geography/geog11.htm (accessed on August 6, 2003).

"Harry Hammond Hess: Spreading the Seafloor." *U.S. Geological Survey.* http://pubs.usgs.gov/publications/text/HHH.html (accessed on August 4, 2003).

"Hayward Fault." *The Berkeley Seismological Laboratory.* http://www.seismo.berkeley.edu/seismo/hayward/ (accessed on September 1, 2003).

"Illustrated Glossary of Alpine Glacial Landforms." *Department of Geography and Geology, University of Wisconsin-Stevens Point.* http://www.uwsp.edu/geo/faculty/lemke/alpine_glacial_glossary/glossary.html (accessed on September 1, 2003).

Impact Craters. http://www.meteorite.com/impact_craters.htm (accessed on September 1, 2003).

"Infrared Yellowstone Gallery." *Infrared Processing and Analysis Center, California Institute of Technology.* http://coolcosmos.ipac.caltech.edu/image_galleries/ir_yellowstone/ (accessed on September 1, 2003).

"Interior Plains Province." *U.S. Geological Survey and the National Park Service.* http://wrgis.wr.usgs.gov/docs/parks/province/intplain.html (accessed on August 6, 2003).

"Karst Topography Teacher's Guide and Paper Model." *U.S. Geological Survey.* http://wrgis.wr.usgs.gov/docs/parks/cave/karst.html (accessed on August 14, 2003).

"Landslide Images." *U.S. Geological Survey.* http://landslides.usgs.gov/html_files/landslides/slides/landslideimages.htm (accessed on August 27, 2003).

"Landslide Overview Map of the Conterminous United States." *U.S. Geological Survey.* http://landslides.usgs.gov/html_files/landslides/nationalmap/national.html (accessed on August 27, 2003).

"Landslides and Mass-Wasting." *Department of Geosciences, University of Arizona.* http://www.geo.arizona.edu/geo2xx/geo218/UNIT6/lecture18.html (accessed on August 27, 2003).

"Lava Plateaus and Flood Basalts." *U.S. Geological Survey.* http://vulcan.wr.usgs.gov/Glossary/LavaPlateaus/description_lava_plateaus.html (accessed on September 2, 2003).

"Major Deltas of the World." *Department of Geology and Geophysics, University of Wyoming.* http://faculty.gg.uwyo.edu/heller/Sed%20Strat%20Class/Sedstrat6/slideshow_6_1.htm (accessed on August 26, 2003).

Mesa in Sedimentary Rocks. http://geology.about.com/library/bl/images/blmesased.htm (accessed on September 1, 2003).

Mesas and Buttes. http://www.scsc.k12.ar.us/2002Outwest/NaturalHistory/Projects/WylieT/default.htm (accessed on September 1, 2003).

Meteorite Central. http://www.meteoritecentral.com/ (accessed on September 1, 2003).

"Meteors, Meteorites, and Impacts." *Lunar and Planetary Laboratory, University of Arizona.* http://seds.lpl.arizona.edu/nineplanets/nineplanets/meteorites.html (accessed on September 1, 2003).

"Mid-Ocean Ridge." *Woods Hole Oceanographic Institute.* http://www. divediscover.whoi.edu/infomods/midocean/ (accessed on August 4, 2003).

"Mississippi River Delta (image)." *Earth Observatory, NASA.* http://earthobservatory.nasa.gov/Newsroom/NewImages/images.php3 ?img_id=9304 (accessed on August 26, 2003).

"Mountain Belts of the World." *Geosciences 20: Pennsylvania State University.* http://www.geosc.psu.edu/~engelder/geosc20/lect30.html (accessed on September 1, 2003).

"Mountain Building Learning Module." *College of Alameda Physical Geography.* http://www.members.aol.com/rhaberlin/mbmod.htm (accessed on September 1, 2003).

Mountains: An Overview. http://www.cmi.k12.il.us/~foleyma/profs/ units/mountains2.htm (accessed on September 1, 2003).

Mustoe, M. *Every Place Has Its Faults!* http://www.tinynet.com/faults. html (accessed on September 1, 2003).

"The New Madrid Fault Zone." *The Arkansas Center for Earthquake Education and Technology Transfer.* http://quake.ualr.edu/public/nmfz.htm (accessed on September 1, 2003).

"NOVA: Mysterious Life of Caves." *WGBH Educational Foundation.* http://www.pbs.org/wgbh/nova/caves/ (accessed on August 14, 2003).

"Ocean Regions: Ocean Floor-Characteristics." *Office of Naval Research.* http://www.onr.navy.mil/focus/ocean/regions/oceanfloor1.htm (accessed on August 4, 2003).

"Ocean Regions: Ocean Floor-Continental Margin and Rise." *Office of Naval Research.* http://www.onr.navy.mil/focus/ocean/regions/ oceanfloor2.htm (accessed on September 23, 2003).

"Okavango Delta and Makgadikgadi Pans, Botswana (image)." *Visible Earth, NASA.* http://visibleearth.nasa.gov/cgi-bin/viewrecord?9152 (accessed on August 26, 2003).

Park Geology Tour: Colorado Plateau. http://www2.nature.nps.gov/grd/ tour/cplateau.htm (accessed on September 2, 2003).

"Park Geology Tour of Cave and Karst Parks." *National Park Service, Geologic Resources Division.* http://www.aqd.nps.gov/grd/tour/ caves.htm (accessed on August 14, 2003).

Park Geology Tour of Sand Dune Parks. http://www.aqd.nps.gov/grd/tour/ sanddune.htm (accessed on August 26, 2002).

"Park Geology Tour of Shoreline Geology." *National Park Service, Geologic Resources Division.* http://www2.nature.nps.gov/grd/tour/ coastal.htm (accessed on August 14, 2003).

Peakware World Mountain Encyclopedia. http://www.peakware.com/encyclopedia/index.htm (accessed on September 1, 2003).

Plate Tectonics. http://www.platetectonics.com/ (accessed on August 14, 2003).

"ReefBase: A Global Information System on Coral Reefs." *WorldFish Center.* http://www.reefbase.org/ (accessed on August 14, 2003).

RiverResource. http://riverresource.com/ (accessed on August 14, 2003).

"Rivers and Streams." *Missouri Botanical Garden.* http://mbgnet.mobot.org/fresh/rivers/index.htm (accessed on August 14, 2003).

"River World." *Kent National Grid for Learning.* http://www.kented.org.uk/ngfl/rivers/index.html (accessed on August 14, 2003).

"Sand Dunes." *Desert USA.* http://www.desertusa.com/geofacts/sanddune.html (accessed on August 26, 2002).

Schultz, Sandra S., and Robert E. Wallace. "The San Andreas Fault." *U.S. Geological Survey.* http://pubs.usgs.gov/gip/earthq3/safaultgip.html (accessed on September 1, 2003).

"The Sea Floor Spread." *Public Broadcasting Service.* http://www.pbs.org/wgbh/aso/tryit/tectonics/divergent.html (accessed on August 4, 2003).

"Slope Failures." *Germantown Elementary School, Illinois.* http://www.germantown.k12.il.us/html/slope_failures.html (accessed on August 27, 2003).

"Slot Canyons of the American Southwest." *The American Southwest.* http://www.americansouthwest.net/slot_canyons/index.html (accessed on August 14, 2003).

"This Dynamic Earth: The Story of Plate Tectonics." *U.S. Geological Survey.* http://pubs.usgs.gov/publications/text/dynamic.html (accessed on August 4, 2003).

Tilling, Robert I. "Volcanoes." *U.S. Geological Survey.* http://pubs.usgs.gov/gip/volc/ (accessed on September 2, 2003).

Trimble, Donald E. "The Geologic Story of the Great Plains." *North Dakota State University Libraries.* http://www.lib.ndsu.nodak.edu/govdocs/text/greatplains/text.html (accessed on August 6, 2003).

United States Coral Reef Task Force. http://coralreef.gov/ (accessed on August 14, 2003).

"Valley and Stream Erosion." *Bryant Watershed Project.* http://www.watersheds.org/earth/valley.htm (accessed on August 14, 2003).

Valley Glaciers. http://www.zephryus.demon.co.uk/geography/resources/glaciers/valley.html (accessed on August 14, 2003).

"Virtual River." *Geology Labs On-line Project.* http://vcourseware. sonoma.edu/VirtualRiver/ (accessed on August 14, 2003).

Volcanic Landforms. http://volcano.und.nodak.edu/vwdocs/vwlessons/ landforms.html (accessed on September 2, 2003).

Volcanic Landforms of Hawaii Volcanoes National Park. http://volcano. und.nodak.edu/vwdocs/vwlessons/havo.html (accessed on September 2, 2003).

Volcano World. http://volcano.und.nodak.edu/ (accessed on September 2, 2003).

"Volcanoes of the United States." *U.S. Geological Survey.* http://pubs. usgs.gov/gip/volcus/ (accessed on September 2, 2003).

Wassman, Cliff. *Mysterious Places: Hidden Slot Canyons.* http://www. mysteriousplaces.com/HiddnCany.html (accessed on August 14, 2003).

"What Causes Landslides?" *Ministry of Energy and Mines, Government of British Columbia.* http://www.em.gov.bc.ca/mining/geolsurv/ surficial/landslid/ls1.htm (accessed on August 27, 2003).

"When Rivers Run Into the Ocean." *Missouri Botanical Garden.* http://mbgnet.mobot.org/fresh/rivers/delta.htm (accessed on August 26, 2003).

"Where Parks Meet the Sea." *U.S. Geological Survey and the National Park Service.* http://www2.nature.nps.gov/grd/usgsnps/sea/sea.html (accessed on August 14, 2003).

"World Geyser Fields." *Department of Geography and Geology, Western Kentucky University.* http://www.uweb.ucsb.edu/~glennon/geysers/ (accessed on September 1, 2003).

"World Ocean Floors." *Platetectonics.com.* http://www.platetectonics.com/ oceanfloors/index.asp (accessed on August 4, 2003).

WyoJones' Geyser Site. http://www.web-net.com/jonesy/geysers.htm (accessed on September 1, 2003).

Index